Flower Power! 6
How to Dry Flowers 8
Say it with Flowers 10

FLOWER POWER!

Welcome to *Flowerbomb!*, a book dedicated to beautiful bloomin' flower projects.

I have been in love with flowers ever since I can remember, from making daisy chains as a young child to choosing the peonies and wildflowers for my wedding bouquet. I find their beauty endless and the joy they bring me immeasurable. My mother studied botany and over the years she has attempted to teach me the names and meanings of an array of flowers; her appreciation has well and truly rubbed off on me.

I am continuously amazed by the design, shape and scent of flowers, and each season brings a whole new set of flora to enjoy. This book aims to pay homage to my favourite blooms through lots of different craft media. I love how using different materials can create such different effects, from felt and wool to leather and crepe paper, and even using resin in an attempt to freeze dried flowers in time.

First comes the Floral Home chapter, full of projects that bring the outside in, which will have you working with all sorts of materials to enliven your pad with blossoms. The Cherry Blossom Vase (page 24) is one of my favourites, taking papier-mâché to a whole new level. I loved making the Pressed Flower Dishes from soft polymer clay (page 32) – they are so useful for keeping my rings in. I'm a big fan of weaving, so I hope you'll enjoy my Woven Aster Hanging (page 36).

Next there's the Flower Fiesta chapter. This brings together some craft and baking ideas you will love. The Frida Flower Crown (page 82) is so pretty for a party or special event. Every party should have a gobsmacking cake and you'll definitely want to try the Flower Bomb Cake (page 62) made with a lavender buttercream icing – it's simply delicious.

As a stylist married to an ex-fashion designer, I have an affinity for fashion and I have so loved scouring the catwalks to inspire the Floral Fashionista chapter. Designers such as Dolce & Gabbana, Versace and Vivetta bring amazingly creative floral designs to their collections year on year. The Flower Bomber Jacket (page 88) shows how you, too, can create a catwalk-style piece by adapting and adorning clothing you already have you. The Wild Meadow Gloves (page 128) are a work of art and the Adieu Bag (page 108) uses embroidery in a modern way to create the most gorgeous handbag.

So what does 'Flowerbomb' mean? Creating a decorative explosion of beautiful flowers across your home and life to bring floral joy to your world!

Flower Power to everyone! x

When you make something from the book, please share it with us! Post your pictures to Instagram using #FlowerBombStyle and tag @couturecraft, @flowerbombstyle and @pavilionbooks

HOW TO DRY FLOWERS

Drying flowers is a wonderful way to preserve seasonal blooms all year round. They can be used for many different types of craft project, from working with resin to decorating candles and adding to soap. Here are a few tried-and-tested ways to dry flowers.

MICROWAVE TECHNIQUE

When flowers are being dried, they release a lot of liquid; using a microwave speeds up the drying process and makes it almost immediate. However, it is best to use the microwave to partially dry the flowers, then use a flower press to flatten them for a few days. The microwave technique is an excellent way to press large flowers, but it's not ideal for very fragile flowers. You can even buy a special microwave press online, but for the method described here, all you need are two flat dinner plates and extra absorbent kitchen roll.

METHOD

1. Make sure your flowers are clean and free of insects: place the flowers in a bowl of water for a few minutes before you microwave them as you never know what's hiding inside. Dry the flowers with kitchen roll. Trim the stem of larger flowers right to the base.

2. Place two to three sheets of extra absorbent kitchen roll on one of the plates and place the flower in the middle. Put two to three sheets of kitchen roll over the flower, then place the second plate on top to sandwich the flower in between. Press down on the top plate.

3. Place the stacked plates in the microwave. If the flower is large, microwave for 1–2 minutes; for a smaller flower, microwave for only 30 seconds.

4. Remove from the microwave and check. The flower will have released a lot of water; change the kitchen roll if necessary and microwave again at 30 second intervals. Once most of the water has been released, remove it from between the plates, place it on a dry piece of kitchen roll and allow it to cool.

5. Finally to flatten, place the flower in a flower press for a few days in between two sheets of blotting paper until flat and dry.

FLOWER PRESS

A flower press is constructed from two pieces of wood with screws around the outside and layers of cardboard and blotting paper inside. Buy a large press as the smaller ones often won't fit in many flowers.

METHOD

1. Collect a selection of flowers. Make sure they are insect free.

2. Place the flowers with good distance from each other on a sheet of blotting paper. (Some people write the names of the flowers and the date when they were pressed on this paper as a record.) Prepare as many sheets as required for the flowers you want to press.

3. Open up the flower press by unscrewing the sides. Ideally, you don't want to disturb the press too much during the drying process, so it's best to layer up your prepared flower sheets all in one go. Starting with a sheet of cardboard, place a prepared blotting paper sheet on top, making sure the flowers are not touching, then cover with another piece of blotting paper. Repeat the layers until the press is full, then screw up the sides.

4. Flowers may need to press for three to six weeks. Open up the press every week to change over the paper, especially for the larger flowers, otherwise moisture will make the flowers rot.

BOOK TECHNIQUE

I once found a four-leaf clover in an old book I had bought; it was perfectly pressed. This is a traditional Victorian way to press flowers. These days it is best to use a heavy book such as a phone directory, something that doesn't matter if the pages are damaged.

METHOD

1. Simply collect a selection of flowers, place in between blotting or parchment paper and put them inside the pages of the book. The more pressure the better: you can balance several heavy books on top or squeeze the book back into a tightly stocked shelf.

2. Check on the flowers weekly, changing the paper as necessary, until they are fully dry.

BRIGHTEN THEM UP!

When drying a flower, often the colour will fade. There are a few ways to counteract this.

Bleach: Wearing a pair of rubber gloves, place the dried flowers in a plastic container and use a paintbrush to apply bleach to front and back. Depending on how much colour you want to restore, allow them to soak for just a few minutes or up to half an hour. Rinse off all the bleach and pat with kitchen roll. Allow to air dry fully.

Citric acid: Wearing a pair of rubber gloves, place a few tablespoons of citric acid powder in a shallow dish and pour boiling water over the top so it is just diluted; stir well. Place your dried flowers onto sheets of kitchen roll and paint on the diluted acid. This will help some of the colour to develop.

Paint: You can paint the flowers once dried to enhance their colour. It's best to use acrylic paint for this.

SAY IT WITH FLOWERS

In Victorian times, posies of flowers were often given as gifts with secret messages. What looks like a pretty bunch of flowers may say so much more! Every flower has a meaning, so why not use their hidden messages to make your craft projects extra special.

I LOVE YOU

Red roses: The deeper the red, the deeper the passion you feel – these are the ultimate symbol of passionate romantic love.

Baby's breath: A symbol of everlasting love – what's more romantic than saying 'I'll love you forever'?

Tulips: These represent the first declaration of love, so if you are saying 'I love you' for the first time, they make an especially meaningful bouquet.

OOPS, I'M SORRY

Purple hyacinth: If you want to say 'Please forgive me', this is the flower for you.

Lily of the valley: Symbolising a return to happiness, this delicate plant is fragile and must be handled with care, just like a relationship.

Star of Bethlehem: This pure white flower stands for reconciliation and a desire to right your wrong, making it the ideal way to say 'I'm sorry'.

THANK YOU

Sweet peas: These say 'Thank you for a great time', making them an ideal gift in return for a meal or evening out.

Hydrangea: These big blooms mean 'Thank you for understanding', a perfect thank-you gift for someone who has helped you through a difficult time.

Bell flowers: These represent pure gratitude in flower language.

Chrysanthemum: Known as the friendship flower, these flowers say 'You are a wonderful friend'.

GOODBYE

Anemones: The name of this flower literally means forsaken, to abandon.

Cyclamen: The meaning of this flower is that all good things must come to an end.

FLORAL
HOME

HULA HOOP WREATH

This giant wreath of joyful flowers will bring a little of the outdoors in, all year around. The flowers are handcrafted from felt and then mounted onto a wooden hula hoop to give this traditional decoration a very contemporary feel. I've chosen a selection of spring flowers for my wreath – pansies, dahlias, blue Himalayan poppies, 'Lauren's Grape' poppies, 'Sun Disk' daffodils and camellias. Why not change the flowers throughout the year to reflect the seasons?

YOU WILL NEED

- A4 sheets of thick wool felt:
    - 1 x bright yellow and bright green
    - 2 x dark and mid purple, off white, blue, dark leaf and light leaf green
    - 4 x light pink
    - 5 x deep pink
- Acrylic paint, bright yellow
- DMC 6-strand embroidery thread, 915 deep pink
- Garden wire
- Large wooden hula hoop, approximately 90cm (36in) diameter

PLUS...

- Fabric scissors
- Paintbrush
- Embroidery needle
- Wire cutters
- Hot glue gun

<u>BUDS OF WISDOM</u> Each flower has a pattern made up of several parts (see pages 138–139). As you will need to make several of each flower type, it's a good idea to make cardboard templates for each flower before you start, enlarging the patterns by 200 per cent. Be sure to label each part of the pattern to identify it easily and keep all the parts together for each flower in a small plastic bag or envelope. Use the templates to mark out the required pieces onto the reverse of the felt as instructed. Depending on the size of your hoop, you may want to make more or fewer flowers in different sizes, or you can simply select your favourites.

TO MAKE A PANSY (MAKE 6)

1. The pansy design can be alternated between having the dark purple or off white (or mid purple) felt as the front colour. For the dark purple design, cut out two small petals from dark purple felt, and two medium petals and one heart petal from off white (or mid purple) felt.

2. On the heart petal and two small petals, paint a semicircle of bright yellow acrylic paint about three-quarters of the way up from the base. Allow the paint to dry.

3. Each petal is completed with deep pink embroidered backstitch lines, three on the small and medium petals, and four on the heart petal.

4. Cut a 20cm (8in) length of garden wire and use the glue gun to attach the petals to the wire: first the heart petal to sit at the bottom, then the two small side petals and finally the two medium top petals.

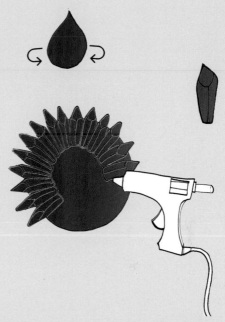

TO MAKE A DAHLIA (MAKE 3-6)

5.   Cut out 38 large petals, 13 medium petals, eight small petals and one base circle from mid or dark purple felt.

6.   To form each petal, simply fold in both bottom edges and glue to make a tube shape.

7.   Glue the first row of large petals around the outside rim of the base circle, then add another layer of large petals. Next add the medium and small petals, and use a few small petals to fill in the centre.

8.   Attach a 20cm (8in) piece of garden wire to the back of the completed flower.

TO MAKE A DAFFODIL (MAKE 8)

9.   Cut five outer petals from off white felt, three inner petals from bright yellow felt, and the stamen from off white felt.

10.   Cut a 20cm (8in) length of garden wire. Run a line of hot glue along the base of the stamen and roll it around the end of the wire.

11.   Use the glue gun to attach the three inner petals to the tip of the wire, overlapping them at the sides. Then glue on the five outer petals to surround the inner petals.

TO MAKE A POPPY (MAKE 5 OF EACH COLOUR)

12. The blue and purple poppies are made in exactly the same way. Cut out five petals from blue or dark or mid purple felt. Cut the central pistil from off white felt and the stamen from bright yellow felt; make the slashes with scissors where marked on these templates.

13. To construct the flower, run a line of glue along the un-slashed side of the white pistil piece and roll this along the tip of a 20cm (8in) length of garden wire. Repeat to attach the yellow stamen.

14. To shape the petals, add a blob of glue at the base of each and pinch to create a frilled effect. Attach the petals around the stamen.

TO MAKE A CAMELLIA (MAKE 5)

15. Cut out five sets of the five heart petal shapes from light and deep pink felt. Put a blob of hot glue at the base of each of the petals and pinch to hold their shape.

16. Cut out the stamen from bright yellow felt, making slashes with your scissors as marked.

17. To construct the flower, run a line of glue along the un-slashed side of the yellow stamen piece and roll this along the tip of a 20cm (8in) length of garden wire. Next, starting with the smallest petals and working out to the largest, attach them one by one to the outside of the stamen.

TO MAKE THE LEAVES

18. Cut out eight poppy leaves from dark leaf green felt, ten camellia leaves from light leaf green felt and six pansy leaves from bright green felt. Attach a 20cm (8in) length of garden wire to the back of each of the leaves.

TO COMPILE THE WREATH

19. Lay the hula hoop flat on the table. Arrange flowers and leaves in a semicircle around the hoop, with extra leaves at each end. Once you are happy with the arrangement, work from each end into the middle to attach the flowers and leaves by winding the wire around the hoop. Hang the finished wreath from a picture frame hook using a small string loop.

TULIP
FOLK
CUSHION

Folk embroidery originated in Eastern Europe from countries such as Hungary and Ukraine. The patterns often depict joyful sprays of brightly coloured flowers in repetitive patterns. This happy-go-lucky design features yellow tulips, which symbolise cheerfulness and sunshine.

YOU WILL NEED
- 2 x A3 paper sheets
- 40cm x 40cm (16in x 16in) cotton twill, white
- DMC 6-strand embroidery thread:
    3 x skeins: 3846 turquoise, 152 pale pink, 310 black, 469 leaf green, 472 lime green, 552 purple, 726 yellow, 906 bright green
    2 x skeins: 112 variegated
- 40cm x 40cm (16in x 16in) velvet
- 35cm (14in) circular cushion pad
- 2 x 2cm (¾in) flat-back gemstones, black
- 24 x 2cm (¾in) felt balls
- Cotton thread to match felt ball colours

PLUS...
- Heat transfer pencil
- Iron and ironing board
- Pins
- Large embroidery hoop
- Embroidery needle
- Fabric scissors
- Sewing machine
- UHU glue

1. Enlarge the embroidery design on page 136 by 200 per cent and print it out. You may need to print it onto two sheets of paper and tape them together from behind. In preparation to transfer the pattern onto the white fabric, draw around the outline of the design using the heat transfer pencil.

2. Make sure your fabric is clean and well pressed, and lay it on top of your ironing board. Lay the paper, pattern side facing down, on top of the fabric, pinning it into place to avoid movement. Using the iron on its hottest setting, press the back of the paper to transfer the pattern to the fabric (this will take a little while).

3. Mount the fabric into the large embroidery hoop. Following the thread guide on the embroidery design on page 136, chain stitch the flowers, the leaves, and the inner and outer loopy circles. Use a filling stitch, such as satin stitch, to create the little circles, and work French knots in the middle of the loops on the loopy circles. I've also sewn a running stitch circle within the inner loopy circle.

4. Once the embroidery is complete, remove the fabric from the hoop and press it from the back. Draw a 35cm (14in) diameter circle on the reverse of the fabric, keeping the embroidery centred in the circle.

5. With right sides together, pin the embroidered fabric to the velvet, trimming the excess fabric from the corners to give a circular shape. Machine stitch around the circle, leaving a 16cm (6in) opening. Trim the seam allowance to 1cm (⅜in) and notch.

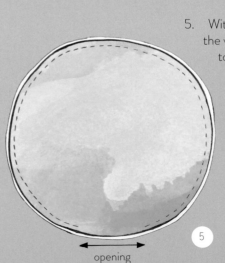

opening

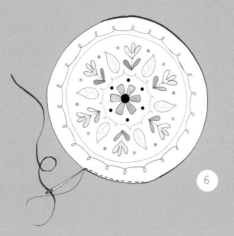

6

8

6. Turn the cushion cover to the right side through the opening and press flat. Insert the cushion pad into the cover and fold in the seam allowance at the opening. Pin, then hand stitch the opening closed. Shake the cushion to create an even shape.

7. To create a puckered effect in the cushion centre, use the embroidery needle and thread to make a stitch through the middle of the cushion. Glue a gemstone to the front and back of the stitch in the middle of the flower.

8. Use the embroidery needle to hand stitch the felt balls, spacing them equally around the outside edge of the cushion.

CHERRY BLOSSOM VASE

Native to Japan, cherry blossom blooms in abundance, signifying the start of spring there and all over the world. This beautifully crafted papier-mâché vase will bring the joys of this season of new beginnings into your home. It is a labour of love, but well worth the end result. Fill the finished vase with freshly cut cherry blossom branches or dried flowers, and if you want it to hold fresh flowers, simply place a smaller glass vessel filled with water inside it.

YOU WILL NEED

- 1 x balloon
- Masking tape
- 30cm x 55cm (12in x 22in) bendable card
- Clingfilm
- 2 x newspapers
- Large bottle PVA glue, or Mod Podge
- 2 x thick cardboard circles cut to 7cm–8cm (3in) diameter
- 1 x A2 sheet of white cartridge paper
- Coarse sandpaper (optional)
- Acrylic paint: white, dark brown, green, crimson
- Gold paint
- Varnish

PLUS…

- Tray or plastic sheet to protect your work surface
- Scissors
- Vessel for mixing glue
- Water
- Paintbrushes: fine and thick
- 1 x A4 paper sheet

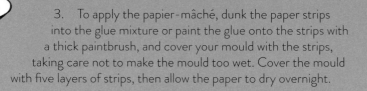

1. To make the vase-shaped mould, blow up the balloon so it is approximately 16cm–18cm (6in–7in) in circumference and tape the card strip around its middle. Cover the mould in clingfilm and place it on your work surface with the flat side down and the balloon on top.

2. To prepare the papier-mâché, cut the newspaper into small strips about 4cm x 8cm (1½in x 3in) and mix up a first batch of glue mixture using PVA glue (or Mod Podge) and cold water (50/50).

3. To apply the papier-mâché, dunk the paper strips into the glue mixture or paint the glue onto the strips with a thick paintbrush, and cover your mould with the strips, taking care not to make the mould too wet. Cover the mould with five layers of strips, then allow the paper to dry overnight.

4. Returning next day, attach one of the thick cardboard circles onto the balloon using a big dollop of PVA glue, to create what will become the flat base of the vase; allow the glue to dry for about an hour.

5. Now mix up another batch of glue mixture and add the next five layers of newspaper strips. Use smaller bits of newspaper to smooth out any creases or join marks and allow to touch dry.

6. To get a stronger finish, add a layer of the white cartridge paper cut into smaller pieces – around 2cm x 6cm (¾in x 2⅜in). As this paper is thicker, allow the pieces to soak for a few seconds in glue mixture until soft before applying to cover the newspaper strips. Take the second cardboard circle, and glue it to the base of the vase and cover with cartridge paper pieces. Keep smoothing out any creases as you go. Then add a final layer of newspaper strips over the top of the cartridge paper layer. Leave overnight to dry fully.

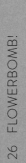

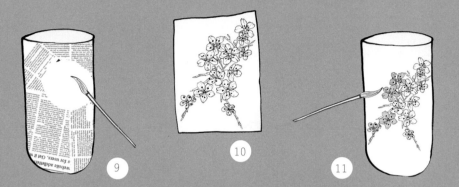

9   10   11

7.   Once the vase is dry, use the sandpaper to get rid of any obvious lines in the paper. Dust off, then paint the vase with undiluted PVA glue and allow to dry.

8.   To pull away the balloon mould, pop the balloon and release the clingfilm from the card. Cut (or tear) around the top of the vase to create a straight line.

9.   Now it's finally time to get painting! Cover the vase with three to five coats of white acrylic paint, depending on how smooth you want the final finish to be. Paint both inside and out and allow to dry in between coats.

10.   Enlarge the cherry blossom illustration on page 135 by 125 per cent and print it out onto a sheet of A4 paper, and cut around the outside of the pattern about 5mm (¼in) from the edge. Paint the back of the cut out design with undiluted glue, ensuring you cover the whole surface well, and attach it to the vase; hold in place and smooth down where necessary for a few seconds. Allow to dry for about 15 minutes before painting over the top of the illustration.

11.   Use a fine paintbrush and the acrylic paint to paint the branch brown, the leaves green, and mix the crimson with a little white to make a pale pink for the flowers. Leave the design to dry before returning to fill in the background with the gold paint.

12.   Once the paint is completely dry, apply a coat of varnish all over the outside of the vase and allow to dry.

DRIED FLOWER PANES

These flower panes are a wonderful way to display your dried flowers preserved in resin. They look truly magical when hung in a window with sunlight reflecting the beautiful colours of the flowers throughout the room. Alternatively, display as a collection on a wall.

YOU WILL NEED
- Small silicone baking sheets (with sides) or silicone Swiss roll trays
- Clear crystal resin
- Selection of dried flowers
- Velvet ribbon, 3mm–5mm (⅛in–¼in) wide

PLUS...
- Newspaper or an oilcloth
- Tray
- Plastic gloves
- Clean plastic container
- Lolly stick
- Tweezers
- Small block of wood
- Twist drill with 4mm (⁵⁄₃₂in) drill bit
- Scissors

<u>BUDS OF WISDOM</u> The silicone baking sheets are used as a mould for the crystal resin and they will need sides to contain it; once used for this purpose, the baking sheets should no longer be used for preparing food. Do make sure you have sufficient resin to fill the silicone baking sheets you intend to use. It's a good idea to create a few panes at a time, as once you have mixed your resin, you cannot store it.

1. Before you begin, protect your work surface with sheets of newspaper or an oilcloth and prepare a space for your resin panes to rest undisturbed for 12–24 hours while they dry. Make sure your silicone baking sheets are perfectly clean and dry. Place your silicone sheets on a tray so that if you need to move them, you can.

2. Now create your design from your collection of dried flowers (see pages 8–9 for flower drying techniques). First draw a rectangle the size of your silicone baking sheet onto a spare piece of paper and start to lay out your flowers as you want them to appear in the resin: a combination of big and small flowers works well, and you can overlap them for more complex designs, or keep them separate for simpler patterns.

2

3

3.   Next, put on your plastic gloves and make up the resin. Follow the manufacturer's instructions to mix together the crystal resin and the hardener in a clean plastic container using a lolly stick.

4.   Pour a 2mm–3mm (⅛in) layer of the mixed resin into your silicone sheets. Next, position the dried flowers on top of the resin using the tweezers. Once you are happy with the design, pour another 2mm–3mm (⅛in) layer of resin on top to cover the flowers. Your flowers may move a little throughout the process but you can use the lolly stick to push them back into position in the first hour of setting.

5.   Let the resin dry and harden fully as outlined in the manufacturer's instructions. Once the resin is completely dry, you can release the dried flower panes from the silicone moulds, which should be easy to peel back.

6.   Make the hanging holes in the top two corners of the pane: place the small block of wood under each corner and drill a hole using the twist drill. Cut a piece of velvet ribbon, thread it through one hole then the next and tie it in a bow. Your panes are now ready to hang.

6

PRESSED FLOWER DISHES

Printing with flowers creates one-of-a-kind patterns on these gorgeous little dishes fashioned from soft polymer clay. The dishes take on a porcelain effect once painted in delicate hues and finished with a little golden sparkle. They are the perfect place to keep your most prized jewels.

YOU WILL NEED

- Selection of hardy flowers (see step 1 for suggestions)
- Small ovenproof bowl or plate
- Fimo soft polymer clay, white
- White acrylic paint and other colours of your choosing
- PVA glue, or Mod Podge
- Metallic gold paint

PLUS…

- Rolling pin
- Smooth chopping board or other even surface
- Scalpel
- Tweezers
- Paintbrush
- Palette knife
- Baking tray
- Sponge

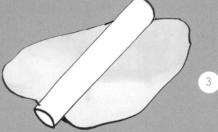

1. First select your flowers for printing: it is best to use hardier varieties that keep their shape and have small or flat flowers, such as baby's breath, wax flowers, cowslips and kangaroo paws. Herbs, such as rosemary or lavender, also work well.

2. Now choose a small plate or bowl to use as your dish mould. The size of the plate or bowl you choose will determine how much soft polymer clay you will need.

3. Manipulate the clay in your hands to soften it before rolling it out on a flat surface to about 4mm (a little over ⅛in) thick, and large enough to fit comfortably in your selected plate or bowl.

4. To make the imprint, place your chosen dried flower centrally onto the clay, then use the rolling pin to go over the top of it a few times to get a good print. Gently peel back the flower to reveal the impressed shape. Some bits of flower may be left on the clay; try your best to remove these using the tip of the scalpel or a pair of tweezers and use your paintbrush to gently dust away any debris.

5. With the plate or bowl upside down, lift the clay with a palette knife and lay it over the top of your plate or bowl mould, ensuring the flower impression is in a good position. Gently push the clay down to take the shape of the mould, then use the scalpel to neatly cut around the outside edge to remove any excess clay.

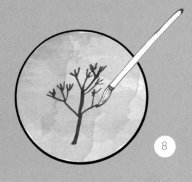

8

6. Place the plate or bowl onto a baking tray and cook in the oven for 30 minutes at 130°C/270°F/Gas mark 1. Once baked, leave to cool completely before turning over to release your dish from the mould.

7. First paint the dish with the white acrylic paint to cover any colour residue left by the flowers. Allow to dry.

8. To get the delicate paint effect, water down your chosen acrylic paint, and give the dish a wash of colour and allow to dry. Then paint over the flower impression with the same (or a different) paint colour, this time not watered down, and wipe with a damp sponge to clear away any excess.

9. Once dry, paint the back of the dish with a contrasting acrylic colour. Leave to dry once more, then finish the edge of the plate with the gold paint.

10. Once you have completed the painting stages, seal the dish by applying a layer of PVA glue or Mod Podge to both back and front.

WOVEN ASTER HANGING

Aster wildflowers come in a variety of stunning colours with an abundance of small petals. In ancient times, they were considered to be enchanted flowers. This abstract weaving, made from a combination of merino and cotton yarns and woven on a small loom, perfectly reflects their beauty.

YOU WILL NEED
- Warp thread, black
- DMC Woolly yarn, 50g (2oz) balls: 2 x green (89), 1 x pink (42), 2 x pale purple (40)
- DMC Natura XL yarn, 100g (4oz) balls: 2 x Guimauve pink (41), 1 x Soleil yellow (89), 3 x Nuage grey (12), 1 x white (01)
- Fluffy yarn, white
- Sewing thread: pink, grey and white
- Dowelling rod wider than the woven panel
- Paint for dowelling rod

PLUS...
- Notch loom
- Weaving/tapestry needle
- Shuttle
- Fabric scissors
- Sewing needle
- Paintbrush

BUDS OF WISDOM The hanging was made on a loom 60cm (24in) high by 50cm (20in) wide. Use the instructions as a guide, sizing up or down to your loom size. You'll start by weaving the flowers at the bottom of the loom, then the work is turned to add the rows of tassels. If you're new to loom weaving, familiarise yourself with the basic principles of Warp and Weft Weaving and Making a Tassel before going on to Weave the Hanging.

WARP AND WEFT WEAVING

1. First set up your loom with the black warp thread: tie the thread on the first notch in the bottom left-hand corner using a slip knot, pulling it tight around the notch. Weave the warp up and over the notches in an 'S' shape until you reach the very end, then tie another slip knot.

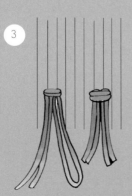

2. The illustration shows how to weave the yarn (or weft) into simple rows using a weaving needle, but this will be easier and quicker if you wrap the yarn around a shuttle. Use the end of the yarn to tie a double knot in the first string of the warp thread. Next, let the shuttle help you separate the warp, so the first warp thread is underneath the shuttle and the second is on top of it, and continue with this in-and-out motion to create your first line of weft. For the return, weave the shuttle through so that the warp thread that was behind last time is now at the front.

MAKING A TASSEL

1. Cut a 40cm (16in) length of yarn and fold it in half. Thread the folded yarn onto two warp threads on the loom with the folded end on top.

2. Pull the ends through the loop to make a sideways tassel.

3. Angle the tassel downwards and trim the ends.

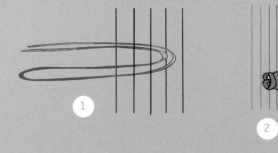
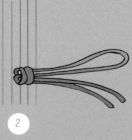

WEAVE THE HANGING

1. Having set up the warp threads on your loom using the black thread (see Warp and Weft Weaving), use green woolly yarn to weave an area about 6cm (2⅜in) high.

2. Next, start to work the first aster flower on the left-hand side of the loom, using the Guimauve pink yarn. Make the first tassel 10cm (4in) from the left edge of the warp. Then tie two tassels above the first tassel.

3. Grow the shape until you are five tassels deep in the middle as seen in the diagram, and then begin curving the tassel shape to form the semicircular base of your flower, at the same time continuing to weave the green yarn into the empty space around the tassels.

4. To make the flower centre, use a small shuttle wrapped with the Soleil yellow to weave a circle at the base of the pink tassel 'petals' using an 8cm (3⅛in) diameter circle cut from spare card as a guide, taping or placing this under your loom to act as a template. Weave the yellow, starting with two warp threads; grow this to four, then six, then back down again to create a circle (this can be adapted depending on the size of your weaving).

5. Tie the tassels around the outside of the circle, butting up to the circle as you go. Once the tassels are about 5cm (2in) deep at either side of the flower, repeat steps 3 and 2 in reverse to make fewer tassels until you have worked just a single tassel. Remember to keep weaving the green yarn in the gaps as you work the flower.

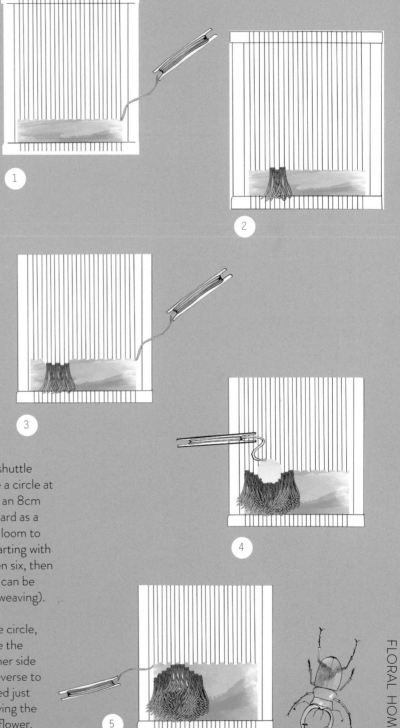

6. Next, repeat steps 2–5 to weave a Nuage grey yarn flower on the right-hand side of the loom.

7. Finally, repeat steps 2–5 to weave a white yarn flower on the left-hand side of the loom. Use the green wool to fill in the area to the left of the white flower, creating a slant in the wool.

8. Now turn your loom so that the woven design is now the right way around. Open up the flowers and trim down the yarn so that all the petals are about 7cm–8cm (3in) long.

9. Now work the rows of tassels beneath the flowers, pushing the tassels up out of the way to work the rows beneath as you go (these will all be pushed back down once the tassel rows are complete, as shown in the diagram). Work the first five-tassel deep section using 40cm (16in) lengths of pink 42, then weave two lines of the same colour underneath and trim the tassel yarn to about 7cm (2¾in) lengths. Continue in the same way to work the white fluffy yarn tassel rows (four deep), then the Nuage grey yarn rows (five deep), working with 60cm (24in) lengths this time and trimming the tassel yarn to around 10cm (4in). Next work a Guimauve pink tassel section halfway across the weave (four deep), filling in the curve and working with 70cm (27½in) lengths; complete the row with 60cm (24in) lengths of the white fluffy yarn on the right (four deep). Trim down the pink yarn to about 15cm (6in) long and the white to about 8cm (3⅛in) long from the previous row of yarn. Weave two lines of same-coloured yarn underneath to secure the tassels. Finally, use four 70cm (27½in) lengths of the pale purple yarn to create the final row of tassels (four deep). Trim the tassel ends at an angle, with the longest on the left about 15cm (6in) from the previous yarn and the shortest on the right again 15cm (6in) from the shorter cut white yarn. Weave four lines of same-coloured yarn underneath to secure.

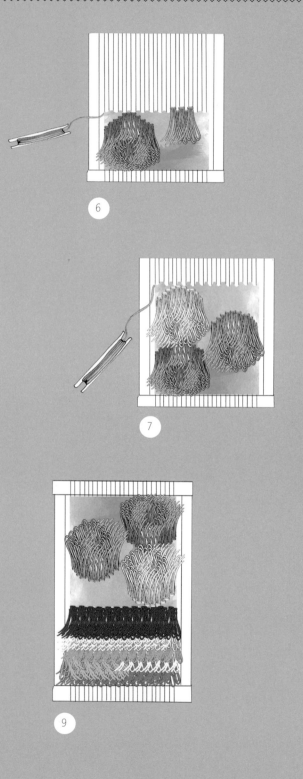

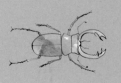

10. To hold the top half of the asters in place, hand stitch the petals to the background using thread in the same colour as the yarn. You may also need to give the tassel yarns an extra trim once they are stitched into place.

11. Paint the dowelling rod in a nice bright colour and leave it to dry.

12. To finish the weaving, use a tapestry needle to weave all the loose yarn ends into the back of the work.

13. To remove the weaving from the loom, starting at the bottom end of the woven panel, cut pairs of the warp thread and tie them together in tight double knots, then stitch the thread ends into the back of the weave and trim. Repeat at the top end of the woven panel but do not trim the thread ends this time.

14. Use the warp thread ends and the weaving needle to attach the hanging to the dowelling rod. Cut a length of warp thread and tie it to each end of the rod to make a hanging loop.

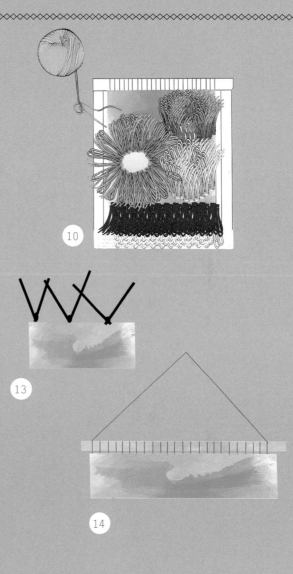

FLORA
TEAPOT

Flowers have adorned teapots for centuries, and this kitchen essential descended from the Yuan dynasty in China, although they drank directly from the spout! This modern take on the classic floral decorated teapot has an abstract design, which means every one will be different. The pattern can be translated to any piece of white china, so you could decorate a full tea set from a teacup to a sugar bowl.

YOU WILL NEED
- White teapot
- Ceramic paint: royal blue and deep pink

PLUS...
- Newspaper
- Disposable cup or old jar
- Kitchen roll
- White spirit or turpentine
- Paintbrushes: fine, medium, and medium flat

1. Make sure the teapot is clean, dry and dust free. Protect your work surface with sheets of newspaper and have a disposable cup or old jar, kitchen roll and white spirit close to hand.

2. Use the fine paintbrush to mark the stems of the flowers in blue. Then use the medium flat brush to mark the leaves. Work your design on the body of the teapot and across the lid, spout and handle, too.

3. Allowing around 10 minutes in between applying colours, add some pink flowers with a medium brush.

4. Once dry, add some blue details to the flowers with a fine brush.

5. Once your design is complete, follow the manufacturer's instructions to ensure the paint is fully dry before using your teapot – some paint needs to be hardened in the oven, whilst others can take up to three days or more to air dry.

ROSE AND VIOLET CANDLES

'She bath'd with roses red, and violets blew,
And all the sweetest flowres, that in the forrest grew.'
Love poems throughout the ages owe much to this verse from
Sir Edmund Spenser's *The Faerie Queene* written in 1590. Let it
inspire you too, to fill your home with the essence of romance
by making these beautiful soy wax candles that will add a
little passion to your mantelpiece or make wonderfully fragrant
gifts for friends.

YOU WILL NEED
- Selection of tumbler-style drinks glasses
- Microwaveable soy wax chips
- Candle wicks, length to suit height of glasses
- Candle dyes: pink rose and lavender
- Essential oil or candle scents: Moroccan rose or rose; violet or lavender
- Dried flower petals: rose petals; violet, cornflower or other blue petals

PLUS…
- Newspaper or an oilcloth
- Tray
- 2–4 x microwaveable jugs or bowls
- Microwave
- Wooden spoon
- Lolly sticks (or skewers/pencils)
- Scissors
- Metal fork

<u>BUDS OF WISDOM</u> It is a good idea to make a batch of candles at a time so you don't waste any wax once it has been melted. Each candle is made of two layers of wax, with dried flower petals being added to the second layer. Ideally you will have four spotlessly clean microwaveable jugs or bowls, one for melting the wax for each section of the red and the blue candles, but two will do at a pinch just so long as you make sure they are cleaned meticulously in between colours.

1. Before you begin, protect your work surface with sheets of newspaper or an oilcloth. Make sure all the drinks glasses are clean and dry and place them on the tray, and prepare a space for the tray to sit undisturbed while the wax sets.

2. Place the soy wax chips into one of the microwaveable jugs or bowls and follow the manufacturer's instructions to melt the wax in the microwave. Use the handle of the wooden spoon to systematically stir the wax as you are melting it.

3. Attach a candle wick to the base of each of the glasses: dip the metal circle of the wick into the melted wax and stick it centrally to the bottom of the glass. Leave it for a few seconds for the wax to cool and the wick to attach, then wrap the top of the wick around a lolly stick (or a skewer or a pencil) and place it centrally over the glass. Trim off any very long ends.

4. The first layer of the wax candles is a solid colour. To create the colour, mix either the rose or the lavender candle dye with the melted wax and stir it with a metal fork until the entire colour has dissolved. If the dye does not seem to be dissolving, put the wax in the microwave for another 30 seconds, then stir again. (If you are unsure of the colour, you can test it by pouring a small amount onto a white plate and leaving it to harden.) Also add a few drops of the essential oil or candle scent.

5. Pour the coloured wax into the prepared glasses so that they are about half to three-quarters full. Allow the wax to cool and harden fully.

⑤

6. To make the layer mixed with dried flower petals, repeat the process to melt the wax, but this time stir in the relevant dried flower petals and candle scent. (Or if you prefer, you could use a clear jelly wax for a translucent layer.) To ensure all the petals don't sink to the bottom of the wax, let them sit in the hot wax in the jug for a minute to soften them. If you do find the petals have sunk, simply sprinkle some more on top of the wax during the cooling process – the cooler the wax, the harder it is for the petals to sink.

7. Top up the glasses with the dried flower layer and let the wax cool fully. Once the wax has completely hardened, remove the lolly sticks and trim down the wicks to around 1cm (⅜in) long.

FLOWER BATH BOMBS

Bath bombs make great gifts and make bath time even more fun. You can experiment by making them in a variety of shapes and an incredible array of scents and colours. These pretty hearts contain delphinium petals, which dry in bright colours and look so beautiful once dissolved.

YOU WILL NEED

- 300g (11oz) bicarbonate of soda
- 100g (4oz) citric acid (follow the safety instructions on the packet when using citric acid)
- 10ml (or 25 drops) fragrance or essential oil of your choice
- Natural food colour (optional)
- Dried delphinium petals or other dried flower
- Heart-shaped bath bomb mould

PLUS...

- Sieve
- Large bowl
- Spoon
- Water in a small jug

1.   Sieve the bicarbonate of soda and the citric acid together in a large bowl. Add the fragrance or essential oil and stir quickly to avoid the mixture fizzing up. At this point you can also add some natural food colour if you wish and a handful of dried petals. Before you add the water, note that you want the mixture to be just damp enough to be able to squeeze together in your hands, and no more. Add a little water and mix to the desired consistency. If the mixture does get too damp, it will keep expanding; if this happens, add more bicarbonate of soda until it calms down.

2.   Take the heart-shaped bath bomb mould and pack the mixture into both halves so that it is just proud of the mould, then squeeze the two halves together. Allow it to dry for 2 minutes. To dry the mixture fully, it needs some air, so carefully remove half of the mould while it is still a little damp (leave it too long and it can be hard to remove).

3.   Allow the bath bomb to harden until it feels solid. This should take about an hour or so, but larger bombs will take longer. Release the second half of the heart and chip off any excess around the joins. Store the bath bombs in an airtight container until you are ready to use them, but remember the fizz wears off after about six months!

FLOWER
FIESTA

HAPPY FLOWER GARLAND

This beautifully delicate crepe-paper garland features Japanese anemones, hollyhocks and foxgloves. It looks gorgeous hung from a mantelpiece and even better trailing at the end of a giant party helium balloon! For great results, be sure to buy packs of best-quality crepe paper.

YOU WILL NEED

- Crepe paper: white, light purple, black, hot pink and green
- Ink pads and colouring pens in pinks and purples
- Fine garden wire
- PVA glue
- Florist's tape, green
- Sugarcraft stamens, small yellow
- Giant helium balloon

PLUS...

- Scissors
- Small sponge
- Wire cutters
- 2 x bowls
- Tall glasses
- Hot glue gun

BUDS OF WISDOM Enlarge the flower petal and leaf patterns on page 140 by 400 per cent and print them out. As you will need to make several of each flower type, it's a good idea to make cardboard templates before you start. Use the templates to mark out the required pieces onto the crepe paper. It is worth noting that this garland will be too heavy to hang from a regular balloon – I used a very large helium balloon. To make the garland as light as possible, be sure to use very fine wire when making the flowers.

TO MAKE AN ANEMONE (MAKE 10-12)

1. To create the petals, cut out five inner petals and five outer petals from either white or light purple crepe paper.

2. For a more realistic effect, dip the edges of the paper petals onto the ink pads and use a small sponge to dab some colour onto the creases in the paper, too; or use colouring pens to vary the tone of the petals.

3. Cut a 15cm (6in) length of garden wire to make the flower stem. To make the pistil, first cut a circle of black crepe paper 15cm (6in) in diameter. Roll a ball of scrap paper about 3cm (1⅛in) wide and put it in the middle of the crepe paper circle. Place the wire in the middle of the ball of paper and wrap the crepe paper circle around the outside of it, twisting the paper tightly around the wire. Trim away the excess paper and wrap the twisted end with florist's tape.

4. To make the stamen, start by cutting a strip of black crepe paper 6cm (2⅜in) deep by 50cm (20in) wide and make small slashes along one side (if your crepe paper is thin, double the depth and fold it in half lengthways before cutting the slashes).

5. Run glue down the un-slashed side of the crepe paper and wrap it around the pistil, wrapping florist's tape at the base to hold it in place.

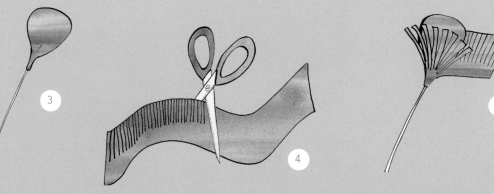

6

6. To finish the ends of the stamen, you need first to make tiny pieces of black crepe paper confetti. Fold and slash a crepe paper strip as in step 4, but this time cut it lengthways too, to give you mini squares. Place the confetti in a bowl and pour some PVA glue into another bowl. Take your flower stem and dip the end of the stamen first into the glue, then into the confetti, and then stand the stem in a tall glass and allow it to dry.

7. Once the stamen is fully dry, use the glue gun to attach first the inner petals, then the outer petals, overlapping them as you go, and stretching and shaping them for a realistic effect. Wrap the base of the flower with florist's tape.

8. Cut out an anemone leaf from green crepe paper and attach it just beneath the flower using florist's tape.

7

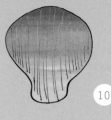

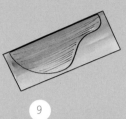

TO MAKE A FOXGLOVE (MAKE 15-20)

9. To create the petals, cut out the petal shape from either hot pink or white crepe paper on the fold. (The pattern can be sized up and down for a more realistic effect.)

10. Unfold the petal and use the colouring pens to make little random spots at its centre. To shape the petal, stretch the crepe paper lengthways at the tip.

11. Cut a 20cm (8in) length of garden wire to make the flower stem. Twist a few of the small yellow sugarcraft stamens onto the tip of the wire.

12. Wrap the petal around the base of the stamen and attach it to the wire using the florist's tape.

TO MAKE A HOLLYHOCK (MAKE 10-12)

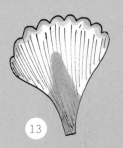

13. To create the petals, cut out five petals from either hot pink or light purple crepe paper. For a more realistic effect, use a colouring pen or the ink pads to fill in a slightly darker shade at the edges and the base of each petal and allow to dry.

14. To shape the petals, pull gently at each side.

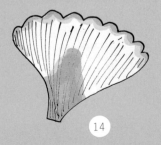

15.	Cut a 15cm (6in) length of garden wire to make the flower stem. To make the stamen, cut a piece of white crepe paper 6cm (2⅜in) high by 4.5cm (1¾in) wide. Coat the inside of the paper with glue and twist it around the tip of the wire, so that the paper is about halfway up; allow to dry.

16.	Attach the petals around the stamen, folding outwards as you go. Place a little glue on the underside of the outer tips of the petals and attach them to one another.

17.	Cut out a hollyhock leaf from the green crepe paper and attach it with the florist's tape.

TO MAKE THE GARLAND

18.	To compile the flowers, organise them on a table or on the floor. Using the wires, attach each flower to one another by twisting the ends around. The foxgloves sit as a collection of flowers and are a nice way to tail off the garland. Drape the garland over a mantlepiece or attach it to the end of a helium balloon. Up, up and away!

FLOWER BOMB CAKE

This skyscraper cake, made with several layers of sponge, is coated with delicate lavender buttercream icing. It is topped with handmade sugarcraft roses and carnations as well as a selection of seasonal edible flowers for an attractive finish. Not only will it blow the blossoms off your friends with its stunning good looks but it will also take their taste buds to a higher level of flora. This cake will serve 12 generously.

YOU WILL NEED

For the sugarcraft flowers
- 24-gauge sugarcraft florist's wire
- Edible glue
- 500g (1lb 2oz) flower modelling paste, white
- Edible dust: pink and purple

For the sponge
- 400g (14oz) butter or margarine
- 400g (14oz) caster sugar
- 2 teaspoons of baking powder
- 400g (14oz) self-raising flour
- 8 x large eggs, beaten
- Lavender extract

For the icing/decoration
- 500g (1lb 2oz) unsalted butter, room temperature
- 1kg (2lb 4oz) icing sugar
- 4 tablespoons of whole milk
- Natural food colouring paste, violet
- Lavender extract
- Selection of seasonal edible flowers (optional)

continues overleaf

PLUS...

For the sugarcraft flowers
- Fondant rolling pin
- Foam pad
- Paintbrush
- 9cm (3½in) five-petal rose cutter
- 7cm (2¾in) carnation cutter
- Sharp knife

For the sponge
- 4 x 18cm (7in) round cake tins
- Baking paper
- Large bowl
- Hand mixer
- Sieve
- Wire rack
- Cake turntable (optional)

- Cake board
- Butter knife
- Palette knife

BUDS OF WISDOM The sugarcraft flowers can be made well in advance of making the cake – the longer the flowers have to harden, the better. They can be kept for up to three months as long as they are placed in an airtight container and stored in a cool, dry place, but it is recommended that you add some padding to the storage container to keep your handmade blooms from breaking.

When making your sugarcraft flowers, work on a clean, flat work surface and have the following items close to hand: icing sugar for dusting, flower modelling paste, sugarcraft florist's wire, edible glue, rolling pin and paintbrush with a little pot of water.

TO MAKE A SUGARCRAFT ROSE

1. Cut a 20cm (8in) length of sugarcraft florist's wire and make a hook at one end. Dip the hook into the edible glue and mould a small cone shape of flower modelling paste around it. Leave overnight to dry.

2. Finely roll out the flower modelling paste onto a lightly dusted work surface. You can make versions of the rose from a bud to a large rose by using one to three layers of petals. Use the five-petal rose cutter to cut out your rose shapes.

3. Place the rose shapes onto a foam pad and shape each one into a petal with the fondant rolling pin. Paint the centre of each petal with edible glue to hold the next layer in place, then take the 'stem' wire and thread it through the middle of the rose shape; paint all the petals with edible glue to attach them to the cone centre. You now have a rosebud.

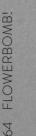

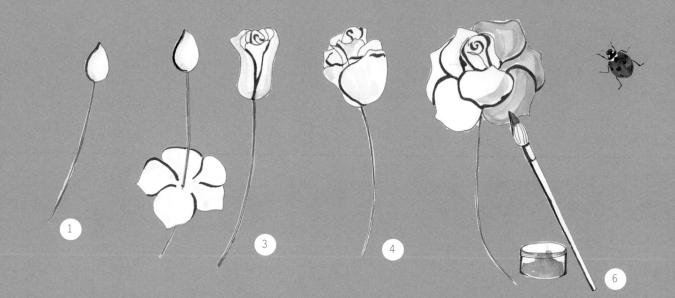

4. Thread the second layer of petals onto the wire, again painting the centre with edible glue. Lightly paint the bases of the petals with the glue and attach them to the central petals, this time shaping them outwards as you go. You now have a small rose.

5. To attach the final layer of petals, paint the centre with edible glue before threading it onto the wire. Press to hold in place, then shape the petals around the flower using the glue to attach them. You now have a large rose.

6. Allow the flowers to harden overnight, then use the edible dust to delicately paint the visible petals.

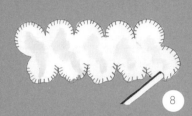

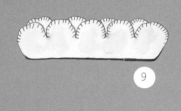

TO MAKE A SUGARCRAFT CARNATION

7. Finely roll out white flower modelling paste onto a lightly dusted work surface and cut out one shape using the carnation cutter. Allow the paste to dry for 3 minutes.

8. Using the end of a small paintbrush, shape the tips of the petals, thinning and rolling the modelling paste.

9. Paint a line of edible glue along the centre of the cut out shape and fold it in half, pressing firmly along the folded edge.

10. Brush a line of edible glue along the bottom (folded) edge of the modelling paste and roll it up tightly from one end to the other, frilling out the petals as you go.

11. To make a large carnation, add two more strips of petals.

12. Allow the flowers to harden overnight, then cut the base of each flower at a slant with a sharp knife. Use the edible dust to colour the tips of the petals.

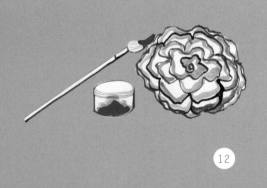

TO MAKE THE CAKE

13. Preheat the oven to 180°C/350°F/Gas mark 4. Grease and line the baking tins.

14. Combine the butter (or margarine) and the sugar in a large bowl and use a hand mixer to mix until pale, light and fluffy.

15. Next, add the baking powder to the self-raising flour and sieve.

16. Combine half the flour and half the beaten eggs with the butter and sugar, and mix well before adding the second half of each. Finally, add a few drops of lavender extract.

17. Pour equal quarters of the mixture into the baking tins – around 4cm (1½in) deep – and bake for 20–25 minutes. The sponges should be golden brown, bounce to the touch and when tested with a skewer, it should come out clean. Turn out onto a wire rack and allow to cool.

18. To make the lavender buttercream icing, cream the butter until it turns pale. Sieve the icing sugar and add it to the butter, then mix in the milk. Use the back of a teaspoon or a cocktail stick to add the food colouring paste and a few drops of lavender extract to your taste.

19. To ice the cake, first layer up the sponges, ideally onto a cake turntable if you have one as this makes the job of icing so much easier. Put a small dollop of the icing onto the cake board (on top of the turntable) and stick the first sponge to it. Spread a layer of icing on top of the sponge using a butter knife, then place the next sponge on top and continue until all four layers are in place.

20. Using the palette knife, give the cake a crumb layer, coating the whole cake in a thin layer of the icing (this will prevent any crumbs from showing through in the final design). Place in the fridge for around 30 minutes to harden.

21. Remove the cake from the fridge and continue to apply the lavender buttercream icing evenly with the palette knife, creating some knife dab marks in the icing for an attractive finish.

22. To decorate, add the sugarcraft flowers to the top of the iced cake. Cut down the wire on the roses to around 4cm (1½in) and stick them into the top of the cake. Use edible glue to attach the carnations. Carefully place the edible flowers just before serving.

WHITE ROSE MALLOWS

The fresh taste of these sumptuous marshmallows brings to mind a summer garden, and the combination of smooth, milky white chocolate with fragrant rose is truly a delectable teatime treat. You can store these treats in an airtight container in your fridge for two weeks. This recipe makes 36.

YOU WILL NEED
- 2 x large egg whites
- 120ml (4fl oz) boiling water
- 30g (1⅛oz) powdered gelatin
- 500g (1lb 2oz) white granulated or caster sugar
- 1 tablespoon of golden syrup
- 200ml (7fl oz) cold water
- 1 teaspoon of rosewater
- Natural food colouring paste, pink
- Icing sugar and cornflour, to dust
- 2 x 180g (6½oz) bars of best-quality white chocolate
- Edible rose petals, small handful

PLUS...
- Electric mixer
- Mixing bowls and jug
- 23cm x 23cm (9in x 9in) baking tin
- Cake release spray
- Clingfilm
- Large knife
- Baking parchment
- Baking sheet
- Spoon

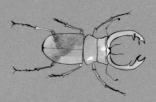

1. Use an electric mixer to whisk the egg whites until they form stiff peaks, then set aside.

2. Measure out the boiling water in a jug, then sprinkle over the powdered gelatin and whisk until fully dissolved, and set aside.

3. Create a hard ball sugar syrup by mixing the sugar, golden syrup and cold water together. Then add the set aside gelatin solution. Finally, mix in the egg whites at full speed for 10 minutes until the mixture turns glossy and is the same consistency as whipped cream.

4. Add the rosewater and pink food colouring paste, and whisk until completely combined.

5. Lightly spray the baking tin with cake release spray and pour the marshmallow mixture into the tin. Cover with clingfilm and allow it to set for around 8 hours or overnight at room temperature.

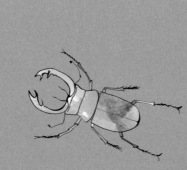

6. When turning out the marshmallow mixture, use a 50/50 mix of icing sugar and cornflour to dust both the top of the marshmallow mixture and the work surface. Use a large knife, dusted with the icing sugar/cornflour mix too, to cut the marshmallow mixture lengthways into six even pieces; then cut each length into six again, to give you 36 evenly sized pieces of marshmallow.

7. Each marshmallow is topped with a white chocolate and rose petal coin for decoration. To make these, start by melting the white chocolate in a bowl over hot water. Lay some baking parchment on top of a baking sheet and use a spoon to drop round chocolate shapes – 36 in all – onto the paper. Sprinkle with edible rose petals and allow to harden in the fridge. When ready to serve the marshmallows, press a coin into the top of each one.

GIANT ROSE PEONY

The 'Julia' rose peony is like a work of art so it seems only appropriate to replicate the beauty of its petals using a watercolour paint wash. This giant version of this stunning bloom takes papercraft flower-making to the next level, creating a wonderful party centrepiece for a special occasion or a glorious accessory for the home to be enjoyed everyday.

YOU WILL NEED

- 1cm (³⁄₈in) dowelling rod, 90cm (36in) length
- Florist's tape, green
- 1m x 1m (1yd x 1yd) crepe paper, yellow
- Elastic band
- PVA glue
- A2 sheets of card:
    - 2 x off white
    - 1 x leaf green
- Watercolour paints: red and orange
- Garden wire, green

PLUS...

- Scissors
- 2 x bowls
- Large paintbrush
- Cup and water
- Pencil
- Craft knife
- Hot glue gun
- Wire cutters

1. To make the stem, take the dowelling rod and wrap it twice with the florist's tape.

2. To form the pistil, cut a circle of yellow crepe paper 20cm (8in) in diameter. Roll a ball of scrap paper about 6cm (2⅜in) wide and put it in the middle of the crepe paper circle, then place it over the top of the stem and tie an elastic band around the base of the ball. Trim the ends of the paper to 4cm (1½in), then wrap with florist's tape to neaten.

3. To make the stamen, cut a 25cm (10in) strip from the 1m (1yd) long yellow crepe paper. Fold the crepe paper strip in half lengthways; run a thin line of PVA glue along the open edges and press closed. Take your scissors and make small slashes along the folded edge to about 3cm (1⅛in) from the opposite side.

4. Run a line of PVA glue along the un-slashed edge of the folded crepe paper strip and wrap it around the pistil, wrapping florist's tape around the base to hold it in place.

5. To finish the ends of the stamen, you need first to make tiny pieces of yellow crepe paper confetti. Fold and slash a crepe paper strip as in step 3, but this time cut it lengthways too, to give you mini squares. Place the confetti in a bowl and pour some PVA glue into another bowl. Take your flower stem and dip the end of the stamen first into the glue, then into the confetti, and allow it to dry.

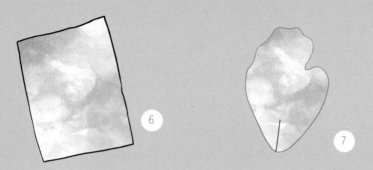

6. To make the petals, first prepare your white A2 card sheets. Use a large brush to lightly paint one side of the card sheets with water, then add red and orange watercolour paint and blend. Once dry, repeat on the other side of the card sheets.

7. Once the card sheets are completely dry on both sides, enlarge the templates on page 140 by 400 per cent and print them out. Mark and cut out five of each of the four different sizes of petals. Cut the central slit at the base of each petal as marked on the templates. (It is a good idea make card or paper templates first.)

8. Use a pencil to shape the petals by rolling their tips backwards over the pencil to create a nice curve, and form the base of each petal by bending the slit edges at an angle outwards and gluing them together.

9. Starting with the smallest petals (petal 1), attach the petals to the stem beneath the stamen. Wrap the base of each petal around the dowelling rod stem and use florist's tape to secure it in place. Repeat this process to attach the remaining petals in size order: petals 2, 3, then 4.

10. Use your prepared leaf bunch template to mark and cut out three sets of leaves from the green card, with one at the top and one beneath at either side rotated 90 degrees to create one shape. Score the middle of each leaf with the scissor blade or a craft knife and fold. Use the glue gun to attach a 30cm (12in) length of garden wire at the back of the leaf, then attach it using florist's tape to either the base of the peony flower or midway along the stem.

VINTAGE POSY TATTOO

In Victorian times, posies were often given as tokens of love and these contained secret messages, depending on the flowers selected. This posy tattoo has its very own special meaning: the single rose represents love; the tulip, true love; and the peony, romance. It looks amazing, yet is unbelievably simple to create and it will wash off easily in the bath or shower.

YOU WILL NEED
- Tattoo paper

PLUS...
- Computer, scanner and printer
- Scissors
- Flannel or sponge and bowl of water

BUDS OF WISDOM Tattoo paper packs have two elements – the tattoo paper itself onto which your tattoo image is printed and a same-sized adhesive sheet allowing you to attach the tattoo temporarily to your skin.

1. Scan the tattoo illustration on page 141 into your computer (it can be sized up or down, depending on where you want to wear it) and print it out onto the glossy side of the tattoo paper.

2. Allow the tattoo paper to cool down and the ink to fully dry, which can take up to 5 minutes. Then remove the protective cover from the adhesive sheet and apply the adhesive to the printed side of the tattoo paper, making sure to remove any air bubbles.

3. Use scissors to cut around the outside edge of the flower tattoo.

4. Apply the flower tattoo to clean, dry skin; get a friend to help you if you want to fix it to a part of the body that you can't easily reach, such as your back. Lay the tattoo adhesive side down in the desired location, dampen the back of the tattoo paper using a flannel or sponge and press firmly for 20 seconds. Slowly remove the backing from the paper to reveal the tattoo and allow to dry fully.

COSMOS STATIONERY

The cosmos flower represents harmony and peace through its perfect symmetry. If sent to a loved one, it symbolises the notion of walking hand in hand through life, which is a beautiful idea. Make your very own cosmos rubber stamps and emboss some notecards to send some good vibes in the post or use them to decorate the cover of your next notebook.

YOU WILL NEED

- 3 x erasers, 5.5cm x 4cm (2¼in x 2in)
- Scraps of strong card
- Clear glue
- Plain notecards or notebook
- Cornflour or antistatic powder
- Clear embossing ink pad
- Embossing powder: leaf green, hot pink, yellow and gold
- Alphabet stamps (optional)

PLUS...

- Permanent marker
- Craft knife and cutting mat
- Pencil
- Newspaper
- Clean sheets of paper
- Paintbrush
- Embossing heat gun

1

2

BUDS OF WISDOM If you haven't used embossing inks and powders before, do a test on some spare card before starting work on your stationery.

1. First make the stamps. Using the template on page 135, copy each of the individual elements – the flower, the leaf and the stamen (circle) – onto each of the erasers using the permanent marker. Working on a cutting mat, use the craft knife to cut away the eraser around the outside of the outlines.

2. As the stamps are quite fine, it is a good idea to mount them onto scraps of strong card. Cut the card just a little larger than the stamp and glue it onto the back of the eraser. Allow the glue to dry fully before using the stamp.

3. Prepare your notecard or notebook for stamping. First, lightly draw a circle in pencil to give you the wreath shape. Protect your work surface with a sheet of newspaper, then dust the card with a little cornflour or antistatic powder before you begin.

4. Starting with the leaf stamp, press the stamp firmly onto the clear embossing ink pad, then press it firmly onto the circle. Repeat, to stamp another leaf alongside the first so the ends are touching. Continue to stamp either three or four pairs of leaves around the circle.

3

5

5. Dust the stamped leaves with green embossing powder and shake off the excess onto a piece of clean paper. Use a paintbrush to carefully dust away any loose powder. Pour the excess powder back into the jar to reuse.

6. Now fix the embossing powder by applying heat with the embossing heat gun. Allow your heat gun to warm for around 30 seconds before bringing it to the card so that it is nice and hot. Hold it about 5cm (2in) from the stamped leaves to melt the powder, but not for too long or you will warp the card. You will notice that the powder changes colour and consistency once melted. Allow it to cool.

6

7. Next stamp a flower over the top of each pair of leaves where they touch, repeating steps 4–6, this time using the flower stamp and pink embossing powder.

8. Complete the flowers by repeating the embossing process to add a stamen in the middle of each flower, using the circle stamp and the yellow embossing powder.

9. To personalise your stationery, use alphabet stamps to add one or more heat embossed initials in gold to the middle of the wreath.

FRIDA FLOWER CROWN

Flowers are used all around the world for different customs and celebrations. During Mexico's Day of the Dead festival, for example, children dance with skull characters decorated with flowers to teach them not to fear death and to appreciate every moment in what is ultimately a celebration of life. Mexican artist Frida Kahlo is best known for her self-portraits in which she often wears a crown of brightly coloured flowers. You can create your very own crown of roses made from luxurious velvet lined with satin.

YOU WILL NEED
- 25cm x 25cm (10in x 10in) thick card
- Crushed stretch velvet (main) fabric:
    - 50cm x 50cm (20in x 20in) dusky pink
    - 50cm x 50cm (20in x 20in) red
    - 30cm x 30cm (12in x 12in) deep purple
    - 30cm x 30cm (12in x 12in) leaf green
- Satin (lining) fabric to match main fabric
- Thread to match fabrics
- 5 x 1.5cm (⅝in) pearl beads
- Wide padded hairband, black

PLUS...
- Scissors: paper and fabric
- Iron and ironing board
- Black permanent marker or dressmaker's chalk
- Sewing machine
- Hand sewing needle

1. Make card templates for the large petal, the small petal and the leaf using the patterns on page 137 enlarged by 200 per cent.

2. Carefully press all the velvet and satin fabrics first, then use your card templates to mark out the required pieces onto the reverse of each of the velvet and satin fabrics. You will need four small petals and four large petals for each flower, leaving space in between to allow for the seam allowance when cutting out (see step 3), so mark eight small petals and eight large petals onto the pink and red velvet and satin fabrics, and four small petals and four large petals onto the purple velvet and satin fabrics. Mark three leaves onto the green velvet and satin fabrics.

3. Now cut out each of your marked pieces, adding a 1cm (⅜in) seam allowance to the outside edges as you do so.

4. Making sure right sides are together, pair a velvet piece with a satin piece and machine stitch along the curved lines of the petals and the leaves. The velvet may move a little, so set the machine to a relatively loose tension setting. (The movement from the stretch velvet adds a little deliberate shape to the petal.)

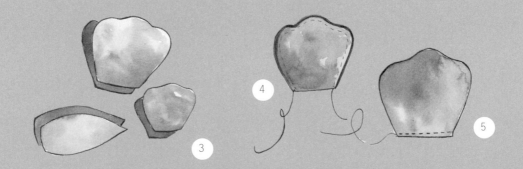

5. Turn the petal or leaf through to the right side and press; on the straight edge, press the seam allowance to the inside, then machine stitch close to the edge.

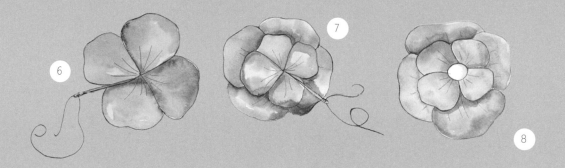

6. To make the rose, attach the petals together, starting with the four large petals. Pinch the base of each petal to create shape and stitch the petals together one at a time.

7. Add the four smaller petals over the top of the large petal base. Make sure all the petals are tightly stitched and that there is no gap in the centre.

8. Stitch a large pearl bead in the centre to complete the rose.

9. Once you have made two dusky pink and two red roses, one purple rose and three leaves, attach them to the hairband: working from the centre outwards, hand stitch each element in place from underneath.

FLORAL
FASHIONISTA

FLOWER
BOMBER
JACKET

Transform a plain black satin bomber into a chic designer piece by sewing sequin flowers - peonies, poppies, daises and forget-me-nots - to bloom across the shoulders and back. With extra pearl and gem bead embellishments for even more sparkle, this jacket is sure to turn heads wherever you go, and it will look just as great with jeans as it does with an evening dress.

YOU WILL NEED

- Satin bomber jacket, black
- Strong black thread
- 1cm (³⁄₈in) flat sequins:
     700 x dusty pink
     700 x red
     700 x gold
- 2cm (³⁄₄in) flat sequins:
     85 x blue
     85 x white
- 100 x 3mm (¹⁄₈in) beads, yellow
- 100 x 4mm (⁵⁄₃₂in) pearl beads
- 30 x small gem beads

PLUS...

- Dressmaker's chalk
- Medium embroidery hoop
- Needle: small enough to pass through the sequins and the beads

TO PREPARE TO START STITCHING

1. First decide where you want the flowers to go on your bomber jacket. For my design, I placed them at the front of the shoulders, over the shoulders and across the back of the jacket in a V shape, but they can be placed wherever you wish, and you can use any colours you choose to make your favourite blooms. It is a good idea to mark out the area with dressmaker's chalk before you get stitching (you can dust it off easily when your design is complete).

2. Once you have decided on your design, place a section of the bomber jacket fabric into the embroidery hoop. It is best to work on one section at a time, from the top of the shoulders down.

TO MAKE THE FLOWERS

<u>BUDS OF WISDOM</u> Each flower is made up of sequin petals and a beaded stamen (or middle bit).

3. Before you start your flower, decide how large you want it to be. The flowers on this jacket vary from 2cm to 8cm (¾in to 3⅛in) wide. To sew the sequin petals, use the needle and thread to stitch down the outside circle of petals.

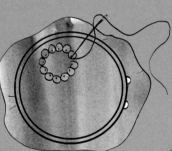

4. Work your way inwards a row at a time, leaving a little circle of fabric at the centre of the sequin flower.

5. Next, stitch beads of your choosing in a tight circle in the middle of the sequin petals to create the stamens.

6. Repeat this process, varying the number of sequins used to make different flowers, until your design is complete.

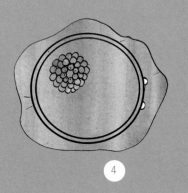

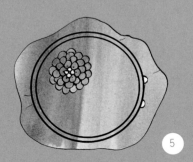

FROZEN FLORAL PHONE CASE

Each of these stunning phone cases is unique. Reminiscent of a stained-glass window, they are a great way to show off the beautiful pressed flowers you have collected on your outdoor adventures by capturing them in resin, fresh as the moment they were picked. You may want to make a few at a time as you can't use the resin again after it has hardened.

YOU WILL NEED
- Selection of very flat pressed flowers
- Clear hard shell phone case
- Clear crystal resin

PLUS...
- Newspaper or an oilcloth
- Clean plastic container
- Tweezers
- Lolly stick
- Medium paintbrush

1. Before you begin, protect your work surface with sheets of newspaper or an oilcloth. Then make a selection from your collection of pressed flowers (see pages 8–9 for flower drying techniques). The flowers you choose need to be very flat with minimal raised sections to allow the phone to fit comfortably back into the decorated case. I have used hydrangea and daisy flowers and rose leaves.

2. To create your design, lay the phone case onto the newspaper with the outside facing down. Use tweezers to place the flowers into the case in the position you would like them, then remove them from the case.

3. Next make up the resin to fix the flowers to the inside of the case. Follow the manufacturer's instructions to mix the crystal resin and the hardener in a clean plastic container and stir using the lolly stick. You will only need a small amount – approximately 50ml (2fl oz) per case.

4. Use a paintbrush to paint a thin layer of resin inside the phone case, right up to the corners. Next, carefully place the flowers and leaves on top of the resin, right side facing down: use the tweezers for extra grip and to move the pieces into position. Once you are happy with the design, leave the resin to set for about 2 hours, checking every so often for air bubbles. If a little bubble appears under a flower, simply use the lolly stick to push the flower down and squeeze the bubble out.

5. Once tacky, paint the back of the flowers with the remaining resin to seal them in. Allow to air dry overnight or for a minimum of 12 hours.

ROSIE SKIRT

This is a stunning couture garment made of layers of beautiful red cotton fabric but it requires just one pattern piece to be custom made to your own measurements. It has a full circular skirt underneath with a top layer of six 'petals' each made from a quarter circle of folded fabric, all joined at the waistband. Give it a swish to see the rose!

YOU WILL NEED
- 1m (1yd) pattern paper
- 6m (6½yd) x 140cm (55in) wide cotton twill, red
- 3.5m (3¾yd) x 140cm (55in) wide cotton, red
- Cotton thread to match fabric
- Heavyweight interfacing: waist length x 7cm (2¾in) high
- 23cm (9in) zip, red
- Hook and eye

PLUS…
- Tape measure
- Pen or pencil
- Scissors: paper and fabric
- Iron and ironing board
- Dressmaker's chalk
- Pins
- Sewing machine and zipper foot

TO MAKE THE SKIRT PATTERN

1. First take the measurements you need to make your pattern (see Taking Your Measurements).

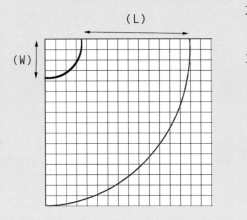

2. Lay your pattern paper out on a large table, making sure each corner of the paper is an exact right angle.

3. To mark the waist circumference, use your tape measure to measure the waist measurement (W) from the top corner along the left-hand side of the paper and make a mark with a pen or pencil. Repeat along the top edge to mark the waist measurement on both sides of the right angle. Then measuring from the corner point, make several W-length marks in between these first two marks, to start to form a curved line. Go over the top of the line to make a smooth curve to give a quarter-circle shape.

4. Now to mark the skirt length: working from the edge of the waist circumference quarter circle, mark the length measurement (L) along the top and side and in between (as described in step 3) to make a second quarter-circle shape.

5. Cut out the pattern with your paper scissors – it looks like a quarter of a large doughnut!

TAKING YOUR MEASUREMENTS
To get a couture fit, following these simple instructions:
Waist measurement: using a tape measure, measure the smallest part of your waist and divide this measurement by 6.28. *Example:* for a 77cm (30in) waist ÷ 6.28 = 12.26cm (4.8in).
Skirt length measurement: using a tape measure, measure from your waist to where you want the skirt to fall. For the skirt to fall just beneath the knee on me, that's 55cm (21.6in); you may want to make your skirt length shorter or longer depending on your height.In addition add 2cm (1in) seam allowance for the hem and 1cm (0.5in) at the waist.
So, the measurements for my skirt are:
W = 12.26cm (4.8in).
L = 58cm (23.1in) – that's 55cm (21.6in) plus seam allowances, 1cm (0.5in) at waist and 2cm (1in) for hem.

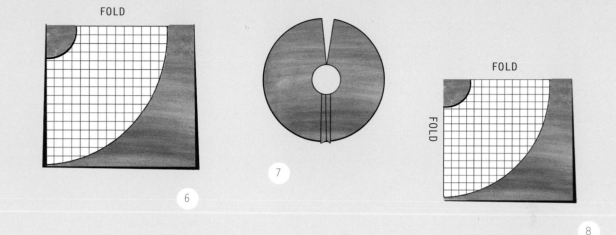

FOLD

6

7

FOLD
FOLD

8

CUT FABRIC AND MAKE SKIRT

<u>BUDS OF WISDOM</u> Make sure your fabric is clean and pressed before you start. First you'll cut out the underskirt from red cotton twill, then the folded quarter-circle 'petal' layer for the top skirt from cotton twill and plain cotton, as the use of different fabric weights creates extra movement.

6. Starting with the red cotton twill for the underskirt, you will need two semicircle fabric pieces for this. Start by making the fabric more manageable to cut: lay the pattern on top of the fabric and mark the length of the skirt, allowing a little room; then cut across the width of the fabric. Repeat this process so that you now have two smaller pieces of fabric (the remaining larger piece of fabric will be used for the top skirt and waistband in steps 8 and 11). Take one of the cut pieces of fabric, fold it in half with right sides together, and lay one straight edge of the skirt pattern on the fold. Use chalk to mark around the pattern, adding a 1cm (⅜in) seam allowance along the open side seam. Repeat on the second piece of cut fabric. Cut out the marked shapes and unfold to give you two semicircles of fabric.

7. With right sides facing, pin the semicircles together along one straight edge and machine stitch together with a 1cm (⅜in) seam allowance.

8. Now use the skirt pattern to cut each of the six top skirt 'petals' from folded fabric, three from the cotton twill and three from the plain cotton. First cut the fabric into more manageable pieces: fold fabric to the length of the pattern and cut along the width, then fold it again widthways to give you two folded edges. Place the straight edges of the pattern to the folds and cut around the inner and outer curves. Repeat to give you six quarter circles of folded fabric.

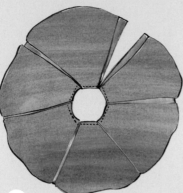

10

9.   Hem the underskirt with a double hem: fold and press under a 1cm (⅜in) hem, then fold over by 1cm (⅜in) again and pin in place. Machine stitch along the folded hem, removing the pins as you go. Unfold each top skirt quarter-circle 'petal' to also hem with a double hem, then carefully refold.

10.   Now attach the 'petals' to the underskirt to form the top layer of the skirt. Lay the underskirt on the table right side up. Pin the 'petals' to the waistline of the underskirt 5mm (¼in) into the seam allowance, bunching them up to space them equally in thirds on each semicircle section of the underskirt and stitch in place. Remove pins.

11.   To make the waistband, cut out a strip from the remaining cotton twill the full measurement of your waist in length by 14cm (5½in) high (in my case 77cm x 14cm/30in x 5½in) and add a 1cm (⅜in) seam allowance all the way around. From the heavyweight interfacing, cut out a strip the full measurement of your waist in length by 7cm (2¾in) high. Fold the cotton twill strip in half lengthways and press, and fold and press under the 1cm (⅜in) seam allowance along each long edge and each short side. Open up the waistband strip and iron the interfacing to one side of it on the wrong side of the fabric.

12.   To attach the waistband to the skirt, open up the pressed seam allowance along one long edge and pin it right sides facing to the front of the skirt over the 'petals'; machine stitch in place along the seam allowance fold line. Remove pins. Now fold the waistband over to the back of the underskirt, pin it in place, and topstitch close to the edge to close the waistband and secure the 'petals' in place.

12

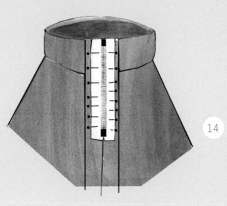

14

13. To close the side of the skirt and add the zip, mark the length of the zip from the waistband down on the wrong side of the underskirt. Pin the two open sides of the skirt together, right sides facing, and machine stitch with a 1cm (⅜in) seam allowance from the hem of the skirt up to this mark. Adjusting the stitch length to a loose (tacking) setting, machine stitch up to the top of the waistband. Press open the seam allowance.

14. Pin the zip from the waistband down, so the zip sits neatly centred in the seam of the skirt. Using a zipper foot on your machine, sew around the outside of the zip, moving the zip pull when necessary to get a straight stitching line. Then unpick the tacking stitches to the base of the zip.

15. Hand stitch the hook and eye at the top of the zip. Turn the skirt to the right side, give the waistband a press and it is ready to wear.

POPPY SHADES

Become the queen of your very own catwalk with these must-have
sunglasses. I've used a fabulously chic pair of cat-eyes for
my base but any big-frame sunglasses would work and this is a
great way to spruce up an old pair. I've decorated mine with
poppies, roses and daises fashioned from Fimo clay, an oven-
hardening modelling clay that is so easy to work with. You can
copy the sunglasses as shown or experiment with the clay to
make your own flower-decorated version.

YOU WILL NEED

- Small blocks of Fimo clay: red, black, white
  and yellow
- Cat-eye sunglasses (or sunglasses with big
  frames)
- 20 x small pearl beads
- 10 x small clear diamanté gems

PLUS…

- Rolling pin
- Small heart cookie cutter, approx. 2.5cm–3cm
  (1in–1⅛in) high
- Small palette knife
- Craft knife
- Baking sheet covered with aluminium foil
- Bamboo skewer
- Superglue or hot glue gun

<u>BUDS OF WISDOM</u> To make the sunglasses as shown, you will need to model the following flowers from Fimo clay: two large poppies, three small white roses, two medium red roses and two small daises. When working with Fimo clay, always warm it up by working it in your hands first, before rolling it out onto a non-stick work surface. (You can create a non-stick work surface by covering a smooth chopping board or baking tray with aluminium foil.) Ensure you thoroughly wash your hands in between working with different shades of the clay as the colour is easily transferred.

TO MODEL THE POPPIES

1. To make the poppy petals, roll out the red clay to about 1mm (less than ⅟₁₆in) thick, then cut out four heart shapes using the heart cookie cutter.

2. Use a small palette knife to loosen the heart shapes from your work surface. Each heart forms a quarter of the flower shape.

3. Lay one heart over the other to form the flower shape, ensuring one side and the bottom tips are touching. Press down at the centre. Pick up the flower and pinch the bottom tips together at the back of the flower to create shape and movement in the petals.

4. Now make the flower centre from the black clay. First, roll a small ball about 8mm (⁵⁄₁₆in) in diameter and set it aside. Roll the remaining black clay into a sausage shape and use your finger to flatten it to about 1mm (less than ⅟₁₆in), then use a craft knife to cut a 1cm x 4cm (⅜in x 1½in) strip. Loosen the strip from the work surface, then use a craft knife to make slashes about 1mm (less than ⅟₁₆in) apart along one long edge. Roll the un-slashed side of the strip around the outside of the small ball, covering the ball with one layer only and cutting away any excess.

5. Press the flower centre into the middle of the petals and press down on the ball to flatten it a little. Use the craft knife to delicately separate the filaments of the stamen.

6. Place the poppy flowers onto a foil-lined baking sheet. Use the bamboo skewer to shape the petals, and use the craft knife to add the lines in the flower centre.

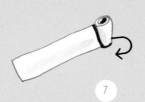

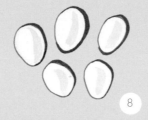

TO MODEL THE ROSES

7. To make the rose centres, roll a small sausage shape from red or white clay and flatten it to about 1mm (less than ⅟₁₆in) thick using your index finger, to make strips measuring about 1cm x 3cm (⅜in x 1⅛in) for the red rose and 6mm x 2cm (¼in x ¾in) for the white rose. Roll the clay strips up from one short end.

8. To make the rose petals, roll five to seven balls about 1.5cm (⅝in) in diameter for the red roses and 8mm (⁵⁄₁₆in) in diameter for the white roses and flatten them into fine petal shapes with your fingers.

9. Take a rose centre and add the petals around the outside, squeezing at the base as you go.

10. Once you have added the desired number of petals, cut off the excess clay at the back of the rose so that it sits flat.

TO MODEL THE DAISES

11. To make the daisy petals, roll out six small balls of white clay and use your index finger to press the balls flat, so that they are about 8mm (⁵⁄₁₆in) in diameter.

12. Lay one petal on top of another to create a circular flower shape, pressing down lightly as you go. Roll a very small yellow ball and place it in the centre.

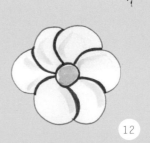

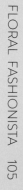

OVEN-HARDEN THE FLOWERS

13. Place the finished roses and daisies onto a foil-lined baking sheet alongside the poppies and bake in the oven for 30 minutes at 110°C/230°F/Gas mark ¼ (or follow the manufacturer's instructions if you are using an alternative clay).

DECORATE THE GLASSES

14. Once the clay flowers have been hardened in the oven and have cooled fully, you can attach them to the frame of the glasses using either superglue or a hot glue gun. (If using superglue, add a small blob to both the back of the flower and the frame of the sunglasses, and allow it to go a little tacky before attaching the flower.) Work from the far outer corner of the frames inwards, attaching a poppy, a white rose, a red rose and a daisy to either side, and a white rose in the centre. Embellish the glasses with the pearl beads and diamanté gems. Allow the glue to dry fully before wearing.

ADIEU
BAG

This beautiful hand-embroidered bag looks like it's come straight off the catwalk. Not just a pretty design, it has a secret meaning too: in the language of flowers, the camellia symbolises faithfulness, the forget-me-not, remembrance, and the daffodil, memories, all joining forces to create a bouquet that encapsulates the sentiment 'when we shall meet again'.

YOU WILL NEED
- 1m x 1m (1yd x 1yd) Aida fabric
- 1 x A4 paper sheet
- DMC 6-strand embroidery thread: 915, 152, 3836, 223, 3705, 760, 712, B5200, 743, 742, 726, 518, 336, 3346, 320, 772, 3078
- 1m x 1m (1yd x 1yd) satin lining
- 1m x 1m (1yd x 1yd) heavy-duty interfacing
- 30cm (12in) bag zip, hot pink
- Bag chain strap, gold

OPTIONAL...
- 30 x 5mm (¼in) pearl beads
- 20 x 8mm (⁵⁄₁₆in) pearl beads
- 20 x 1cm (³⁄₈in) bugle beads
- Gold jewellery wire

PLUS...
- Heat transfer pencil
- Iron and ironing board
- Extra large embroidery hoop
- Needles: embroidery and sewing
- Pencil and metal ruler
- Scissors: fabric and embroidery
- Sewing machine and zipper foot
- Pins
- Wire cutters and flat-nose pliers (optional)

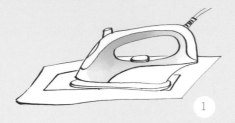

1. Cut the Aida fabric in half and set one piece aside for the bag back. Transfer the embroidery pattern onto the other half of the Aida fabric. Enlarge the reversed embroidery pattern on page 132 by 125% per cent and print it out onto the A4 paper sheet, then use an iron-on pattern pencil to draw over the outlines of the floral design. Turn the paper over and place in the centre of the fabric; use a hot iron to press down onto the back of the paper and hold in place for a few seconds to transfer the image to the fabric.

2. Mount the fabric into the embroidery hoop so that the floral design is centred. Using a filling stitch, such as satin stitch, embroider the design referring to the thread guide diagram on page 133. Complete the embroidery by adding the French knot details to the centre of the peony and the forget-me-nots (see photo, page 113).

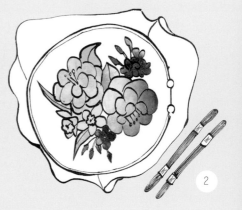

3. Remove the completed embroidery from the hoop, trim away any excess threads from the back, and press on the reverse.

4. Mark out the basic bag shape on the back of the embroidery. Use a pencil and ruler to draw a rectangle 32cm (12½in) wide by 24cm (9½in) high, ensuring the floral motif is centred within this area. Cut out adding a 1cm (⅜in) seam allowance around the outside.

5. Use the embroidered front panel as a template to cut out the bag back from the set aside Aida fabric and to cut two pieces each from the satin lining fabric and the interfacing.

24cm (9½in)

32cm (12½in)

4

6. Make a bag side pattern from a spare piece of thin card: this is a triangle measuring 12cm (4¾in) wide at its base by 24cm (9½in) high. Use the bag side pattern to mark out two triangles each onto the Aida fabric, the satin lining and the interfacing, and cut out adding a 1cm (⅜in) seam allowance.

7. For the base of the bag, mark out a rectangle measuring 32cm (12½in) wide by 12cm (4¾in) high onto the Aida fabric, the satin lining and the interfacing, and cut out adding a 1cm (⅜in) seam allowance.

8. Use a hot iron to apply the interfacing pieces (shiny side down) to the back of all the Aida fabric pieces.

9. To make the strap loops, start by cutting out two pieces measuring 4cm x 10cm (1½in x 4in) from the remaining Aida fabric. Press each strip in half lengthways, then unfold and press each long side into the middle fold line; fold the strip in half lengthways once again, press and machine stitch closed along the edge. Fold each completed strip in half to make a loop and attach the loops to the bag sides 4cm (1½in) down from the top point of the triangle, sewing over the ends of the loops several times to ensure that they are firmly attached.

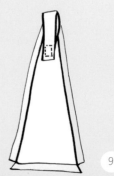

9

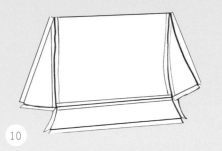

10

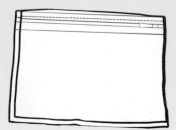

11

10. To make up the bag, begin by machine stitching the outer (Aida) fabric sides and base to the embroidered front of the bag, pinning the pieces together before stitching along the seam allowance. Repeat to make a matching lining panel from the satin fabric pieces.

11. Place the embroidered front (with attached sides and base) so that the right side is facing up. Then position the zip right side facing down to align with the top of the fabric, with the zip pull to the left, and pin it along the top edge. Place the matching lining panel on top with the right side facing down; align at the top edge and re-pin. (The zip shown in red in the diagram is sandwiched in between the Aida and lining fabric so can't be seen.)

12. Using a zipper foot, machine stitch a straight line close to the edge of the zip. When you get to the zip pull, move it along to continue to sew in a straight line to the end. Fold both sides back so that the Aida and lining fabrics are wrong sides facing and press (see diagram).

13. To make the other (back) side of the bag, place the back Aida fabric panel right side facing up. Take the front panel (from step 12) and lay it on top with satin (lining) side up, aligning the unstitched edge of the zip at the top edge. Now lay the satin lining back piece on top with the right side facing down, again aligning the top edges, and sew in place as in step 12.

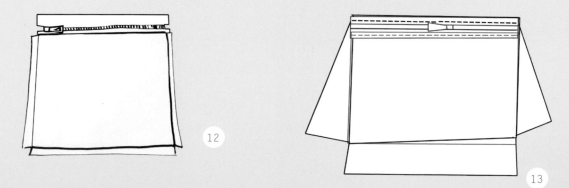

12

13

14

14. Open up the bag and press along the zip line. Then top stitch close to the edge of the zip to give a neat finish.

15. To complete the stitching of the bag, open up the sides and, with right sides facing, pin lining to lining and outer fabric to outer fabric. (The zip pull needs to be in the middle of the zip to turn out.) Machine stitch along the 1cm (⅜in) seam allowance, leaving a 10cm (4in) opening at the bottom of the lining fabric to pull the bag through.

16. Pull the bag through the opening and double check that the zip sides are lined up correctly. Once you are happy, clip the corners and trim the seam allowance to 5mm (¼in). Pull the bag back through the opening, push out the corners in the outer fabric, then hand or machine stitch the opening closed. Push the lining back inside the bag and give it a good press.

17. Attach the gold chain strap to the strap loops. Your bag is now complete, but for that extra special finish, you can add pearl and bugle beads to the embroidery if you choose and bead link embellishments to the chain.

17

HYDRANGEA BLOOM SWEATER

This sweater looks like it's straight out of a floral wonderland. The tiny flowers that make the pompom balls of a hydrangea come in the most beautiful colours and are easy to replicate in crochet to sit perfectly on the shoulders of a knitted jumper. The crochet pattern is simple to do, even for a novice, so get ready to flowerbomb your knitwear and create your own couture masterpiece in the process.

YOU WILL NEED
- Knitted jumper
- DMC Natura Yarn, 100g (4oz) balls:
  1 x Amaranto (N33), 1 x Agatha (N44),
  1 x Lobelia (N82)
- DMC Natura XL Yarn, 100g (4oz) balls:
  1 x Guimauve pink (41), 1 x Ecru
- Thread to match yarn colours
- 16 x 1.5cm (⅝in) pearl beads
- 12 x large silver gemstones

PLUS...
- Crochet hooks: 3mm (C2 or D3) and 6mm (J10)
- Needle
- Hot glue gun (optional)

BUDS OF WISDOM If you're a crochet novice, follow To Make a Crochet Flower and the step-by-step photos, which show the working of a small flower. (If you can crochet already, skip to the abbreviated pattern text on page 119.) The crochet flower is made of a central ring to which the petals are attached. The process of making the flower is the same for both small and large versions, but the number of stitches is scaled up for the larger one (see page 119). You'll need about 50 small and 28 large flowers in all.

TO MAKE A CROCHET FLOWER

1. Using a 3mm crochet hook and 4-ply yarn, make a slip knot to create a loop. Start to create a chain by pulling the yarn through the loop with your hook. Chain 6. Join the ends of the chain together using a slip stitch to create a circle.

2. Chain 3.

3. Work a treble crochet through the centre ring of the flower: wrap the yarn around the hook twice, then pass it through the centre of the circle, wrap the yarn over the hook once and pull it through the hole.

4. Pass the yarn over the end of the hook again and pull it through two of the loops.

5. Wrap the yarn around again and pull it through the two loops...

6. ...to end up with one loop to complete the treble crochet stitch.

7. Repeat steps 3–6 twice more to make a total of 3 treble crochet stitches. Chain 3.

8. Attach to the circle using a slip stitch.

9. Chain 3 in preparation to make a second petal.

10. Create each petal – you'll make a total of four in the same way. When you have completed four petals, tie the yarn in a knot and trim the end.

CROCHET TERMINOLOGY
The small and large flower crochet patterns are written using UK crochet terms, which differ slightly from terminology used in the US, as outlined below:

UK	US
treble crochet	double crochet
triple treble crochet	double treble crochet

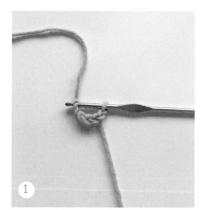

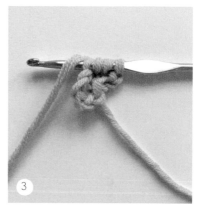

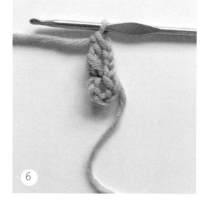

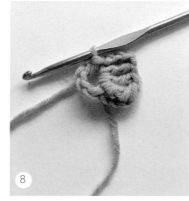

PATTERN FOR SMALL FLOWER (MAKE 50)

Using a 3mm crochet hook and 4-ply yarn in a colour of your
    choosing, make a slip knot.
Chain 6.
Join the ends of the chain together with a slip stitch through
    the first chain.

To make the petals

Chain 3.
Work 3 treble crochet stitches through the centre ring.
Chain 3.
Slip stitch through the centre.
Repeat to make a total of 4 petals and tie knot after last petal.
Trim away loose threads.

PATTERN FOR LARGE FLOWER (MAKE 28)

Using a 6mm crochet hook and super chunky yarn in a colour
    of your choosing, make a slip knot.
Chain 7.
Join the ends of the chain together with a slip stitch through
    the first chain.

To make the petals

Chain 5.
Work 4 triple treble crochet stitches through the centre ring.
Chain 3.
Slip stitch through the centre.
Repeat to make a total of 4 petals and tie knot after last petal
Trim away loose threads.

TO ATTACH AND FINISH THE FLOWERS

Once you have completed sufficient flowers, stitch
them onto the jumper to cover the shoulders front
and back using a thread to match the yarn. Stitch the
pearl beads and gemstones to the centre of the larger
flowers to finish; alternatively, use a hot glue gun to fix
them in place.

WORKING TRIPLE TREBLE CROCHET STITCHES

New to crochet? Follow these
instructions for working a triple treble
crochet stitch:
Wrap the yarn around the hook (yarn
    over) three times and insert the hook
    through centre of circle. Yarn over
    and pull through the circle (five loops
    on hook).
Yarn over and pull through two loops (four
    loops on hook).
Yarn over and pull through two loops
    (three loops on hook).
Yarn over and pull through two loops (two
    loops on hook).
Yarn over and pull through two loops to
    leave one loop on the hook.

KILLER HEELS

The inspiration for this pair of 'killer' heels is, appropriately, the poisonous hellebore flower, and more specifically, the dramatically flamboyant hellebore 'Black Swan'. The name 'Helleborus' derives from the Greek 'elein' meaning 'to injure' and 'bora' meaning 'food', adding up to a taste of poison. According to folklore, the hellebore flower was an ingredient in the legendary 'witches' flying ointment' and it has a long association with witchcraft.

YOU WILL NEED
- Pair of mules
- Thin leather or leatherette, black
- Black thread
- 60 x 3mm (⅛in) pearl beads
- 60 x 4mm (⁵⁄₃₂in) flat sequins, gold
- 60 x 2cm (¾in) bugle beads, black
- 60 x headpins, gold
- 6 x 1.5cm (⅝in) flat-back gemstones,
- 80 x 5mm (¼in) flat-back gemstones, black

PLUS...
- Sharp fabric scissors
- Strong, sharp leather needle
- Flat-nose pliers
- Wire cutters
- Hot glue gun

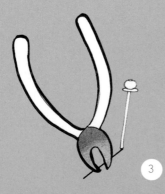

1. Each shoe is decorated with three flowers, two large and one small. Use the petal pattern on page 137 to make template from scrap card. Use the card template to mark out 28 petals on the back of the black leatherette (that's five petals for each of the two larger flowers and four petals for the smaller flower per shoe). Cut out the petals using sharp scissors.

2. Working on one petal at a time, pinch the base (rounded end) of the petal together to create a fold in the middle and a nice curved shape at the sides, then stitch in position. Put the petals aside.

3. To create the stamens, thread one pearl, one gold sequin and one bugle bead onto a headpin. Bend the pin at the base to a right angle and snip off the wire to 1cm (⅜in) long. You will need about eight to ten stamens per flower, approximately 50–60 in total.

4. Next, use the glue gun to attach the petals to the shoes. Run a line of glue along the widest part of the underside of the petals (you need the base of the petal to be left unglued to be able to attach the stamens in the middle of the flower in step 5). Glue the petals in place to make a five-petal flower on the outer side and the front of each shoe and a smaller four-petal flower on the inner side.

5. To attach the stamens, run a line of glue along the wire at the base of each stamen and stick them under the unglued edge at the base of the petals. Use about eight to ten per flower to make a circle of stamens in the middle of the flower around 1.5cm (⅝in) wide. Glue a large flat-back gemstone to the middle of each flower, pushing it down firmly and holding it for a few seconds to make sure it is securely attached.

6. Decorate the spaces between the flowers with the smaller flat-back gemstones, creating curved lines to represent stems and leaves. Glue in place and leave around a 3mm (⅛in) gap in between stones.

DAISY CHAIN NECKLACE

Daisies and anemones grow in the spring. The daisy actually grows in every country in all the continents of the world except Antarctica! A daisy chain is a symbol of youth and purity and the anemone is said to be a lucky charm. What better reason then to make this beautiful necklace.

YOU WILL NEED

- 1 x A4 sheet of craft aluminium (0.14mm thick)
- Radiator enamel paint: white, black and pink
- 5 x 18mm (¾in) flat-back gemstones, black
- 5 x plain bezel connector beads or flat round beads
- 50cm (20in) jewellery chain
- 12 x 6mm (¼in) jump rings
- Necklace clasp

PLUS…

- Sharp scissors
- Newspaper
- White spirit in disposable cup
- Old cloth or kitchen towel
- 3 x paintbrushes
- Superglue
- Wire cutters
- Round-nose pliers

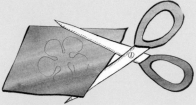

1. Using the daisy and anemone flower templates on page 134, mark out three large daisies, three small daisies, two large anemones and four small anemones onto the sheet of craft aluminium, and cut out the flowers using a sharp pair of scissors.

○1

2. Cover your worktop with sheets of newspaper and place a disposable cup with white spirit in it and an old cloth nearby in case of spills. Lay the flowers onto the newspaper and, using a different paintbrush for each colour, cover all the daisies with the white enamel paint, the large anemones with the black and the small anemones with the pink. They will need two to three coats, front and back. Allow to dry in between coats.

○2

3. Once the flowers are dry, shape the petals by curving them inwards with your fingers. Then use superglue to attach the flower layers. For the daises, glue the small daisy flowers to the large daisy flowers. For the anemones, glue two small pink anemone flowers onto each large black anemone flower, ensuring that the petals are staggered and not directly on top of one another. Glue a gemstone in the middle of each flower. Allow the glue to dry completely before moving on.

4. Once the glue has fully dried, glue the plain bezel connector beads to the centre back of each of the flowers. For a better finish, you can paint over them with enamel paint, but this is not essential.

○4

5. To make the necklace, first use the wire cutters to cut four pieces of chain measuring 4cm (1½in) and two pieces measuring 14cm (5½in). Starting with a 14cm (5½in) piece, attach a jump ring to the end of the chain and attach it to one side of the bezel connector bead on one of the daisies using round-nose pliers, then add another jump ring to the other side of the bezel connector and add a 4cm (1½in) piece of chain. At the end of this chain, add another jump ring, then an anemone and so on, alternating flowers and finishing with the second piece of 14cm (5½in) chain.

6. To complete the necklace, add the necklace clasp to each end of the chain.

WILD MEADOW GLOVES

In spring and summertime, meadows are abundant with wildflowers, buttercups, daisies, blue flax and clover to name but a few, and they make for an amazing tapestry of colour. These gloves celebrate the gorgeous array of nature's wildflowers using leatherette, felt, sequins and beads.

YOU WILL NEED
- Thin leatherette: yellow and bright pink
- Thick wool felt: light blue and mid blue
- Pair of long leather or leatherette gloves
- Thread to match felt, leatherette and gloves
- 2 x 1.5cm (⅝in) sequin flowers, blue
- 4 x flower beads, gold
- 4 x 5mm (¼in) pearl beads
- 12 x 2cm (¾in) flat sequins, white
- 12 x 1cm (⅜in) sequins, gold
- 50 x 8mm (⁵⁄₁₆in) flat bugle beads, gold
- 18 x small flower sequins, silver or white
- 18 x 3mm (⅛in) gemstones, pink and blue

PLUS...
- Pencil
- Fabric scissors
- Stiff card
- Needle, strong enough to get through your fabric
- Fabric glue
- Clear shoe protector (optional)

1. Transfer the petals and leaf templates on page 137 to scraps of thin card and use to cut out the pieces from the leatherette and felt that you will need to make the flowers (see steps 2–6 for details).

2. Before starting to sew, place a piece of stiff cardboard inside each glove; this will prevent you from stitching through to the back of the glove. Begin with the flower closest to the fingers, then work your way up to the wrist. The first flower, a yellow clover, sits just above the little finger. It consists of five medium yellow leatherette petals with a blue sequin flower in the centre. Pinch the middle of the petals and stitch onto the fabric, working in a circle and securing with a knot to finish. Once the flower is complete, attach the blue sequin flower to its centre using either a little fabric glue or by stitching it in place.

3. The next flower, a meadow cranesbill, consists of five medium petals in light blue felt, five small petals in mid blue felt and a gold flower bead in the centre, topped with a pearl. Attach all elements as before.

4. Next stitch the large yellow clover flower, consisting of five large yellow leatherette petals with a centre made from six 2cm (¾in) white sequins and six 1cm (⅜in) gold sequins, topped with a pearl.

5. The final flower, a pink cranesbill, is made using five medium pink leatherette petals with a gold flower bead in the centre, topped with a gemstone.

6. Now stitch the five mid blue felt leaves in place, one behind the small yellow clover and four behind the large yellow clover.

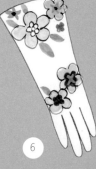

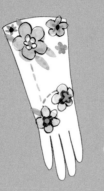

(7)

7. Next stitch the bugle bead tendrils, starting with the one between the small and large yellow clover flowers. Using a thread colour to match your gloves, bring your needle up under one of the small clover petals, thread on the number of bugle beads required to complete the tendril and take the needle back under one of the petals of the large clover. Then stitch over the top of the bugle beads back down to the small clover flower, keeping close to the base of the beads. Work the bugle bead tendril between the small yellow clover and the cranesbill in the same way.

8. Fill in any empty spaces with the little flower sequins topped with the small gemstones. To protect the gloves from the rain, lightly spray them with clear shoe protector.

(8)

TEMPLATES AND GUIDES

Use the templates below, enlarging if advised, to make the projects. Alternatively, download the templates from www.pavilionbooks.com/flowerbomb

ADIEU BAG (PAGE 108)

Embroidery Pattern
(reversed)
Enlarge by 125%

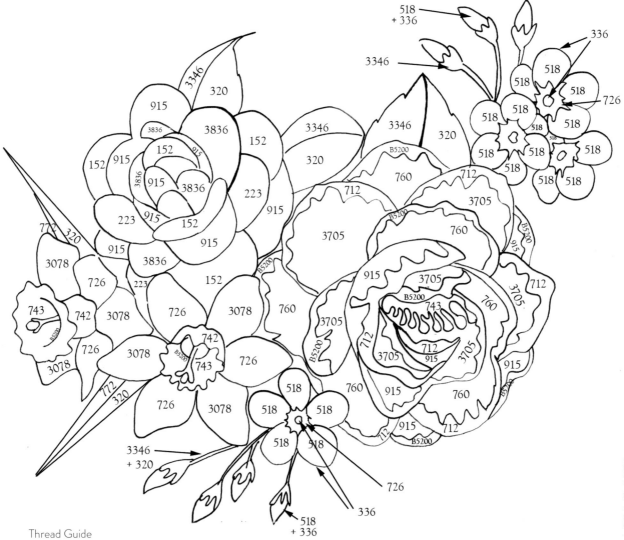

Thread Guide

Large Daisy

Small Daisy

Small Anemone

Large Anemone

**CHERRY BLOSSOM VASE
(PAGE 24)**
Enlarge by 125%

**COSMOS
STATIONERY
(PAGE 78)**
Cosmos Flower Stamp

Petal

Leaf

Stamen

TULIP FOLK CUSHION (PAGE 20)

Embroidery Pattern and Thread Guide
Enlarge by 200%

FRIDA FLOWER CROWN (PAGE 82)
Enlarge by 200%

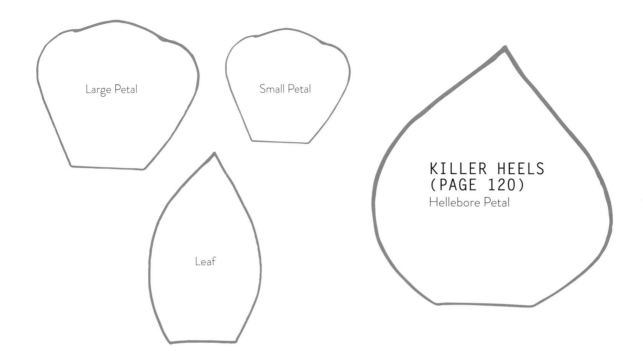

Large Petal

Small Petal

Leaf

KILLER HEELS
(PAGE 120)
Hellebore Petal

WILD MEADOW GLOVES (PAGE 128)

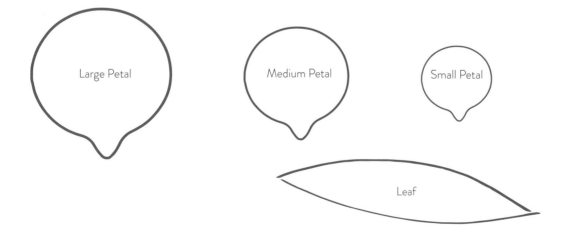

Large Petal

Medium Petal

Small Petal

Leaf

HULA HOOP WREATH (PAGE 14)

Enlarge by 200%

DAFFODIL

Outer Petal
x 5

Inner Petal
x 3

Stamen
x1

PANSY

Heart Petal
x 1

Medium Petal
x 2

Small Petal
x 2

Pansy Leaf
x 6

DAHLIA

Large Petal
x 38

Medium Petal
x 13

Small Petal
x 8

Base Circle x 1

CAMELLIA

Petal
x 5

Petal
x 5

Stamen
x 1

Petal
x 5

Petal
x 5

Camellia Leaf
x 10

Petal
x 5

POPPY

Petal
x 5

Pistil
x 1

Poppy Leaf
x 8

Stamen
x 1

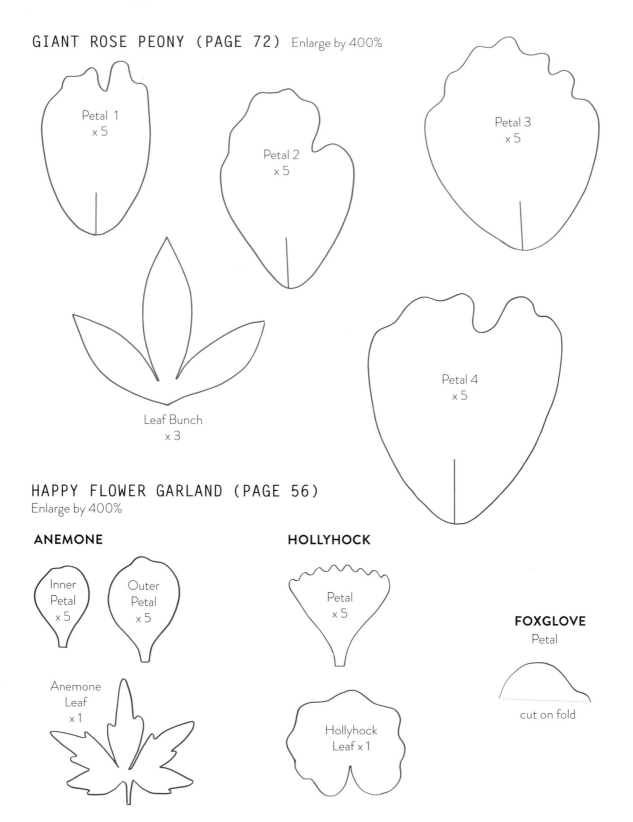

GIANT ROSE PEONY (PAGE 72) Enlarge by 400%

Petal 1
x 5

Petal 2
x 5

Petal 3
x 5

Leaf Bunch
x 3

Petal 4
x 5

HAPPY FLOWER GARLAND (PAGE 56)
Enlarge by 400%

ANEMONE

Inner
Petal
x 5

Outer
Petal
x 5

Anemone
Leaf
x 1

HOLLYHOCK

Petal
x 5

Hollyhock
Leaf x 1

FOXGLOVE
Petal

cut on fold

VINTAGE POSY TATTOO
(PAGE 76)

SUPPLIERS

GENERAL CRAFT
Hobbycraft.co.uk
Hobbycraft supply a huge range of crafting materials and, with friendly staff in store and an easy to navigate website, they are the best place to find all your general craft needs.

SEWING
Janome.co.uk
Janome are a leading **sewing machine** supplier and they create best quality domestic machines. All the projects in this book were sewn on the DSK100 model.

Dmccreative.co.uk
DMC provides premium quality **yarns and embroidery threads** in every colour imaginable. I have referenced the exact colours used for their yarns and embroidery threads for the projects in this book.

Cloudcraft.co.uk
Cloud Craft have a beautiful website and supply premium quality **wool felt** in a delicious range of colours. As well as this, they have an excellent range of trims and craft kits.

Simplysequins.co.uk
Simply Sequins have the most incredible range of **sequins** online. They stock more varieties than you can imagine, a bit like an Aladdin's cave.

CLAY
Staedtler.co.uk
Fimo clay is a wonderful oven-hardening clay that comes in an array of colours. Incredibly versatile to use, it can be used for so many different craft projects.

ACKNOWLEDGEMENTS

Wow what a bloomin' beautiful book to work on.

First and foremost thanks to my two bears, daddy bear and baby bear, as always you are my world. My mother, for teaching me so much about flowers growing up, and my dad, for showing me which ones were weeds…

I have had a floral book boiling in the back of my head for a few years now, and the team at Pavilion loved the idea, too! Thank you to Polly and Katie for believing in this book. To my editors Krissy and Cheryl and designers Michelle and Sophie, thank you for working with me so closely to get this baby exactly how we wanted it. Thanks to lovely Tiffany Mumford for the fabulous floral photos; I always love working with you. Thanks also to Amy Christian and Ione Walder for being there at the beginning.

A huge thank you to all my superstar suppliers who have made this book possible: Hobbycraft, Janome, DMC, Cloud Craft, Simply Sequins and Staedtler. All the materials in this book have come from these sponsors, so look no further.

ABOUT HANNAH

Hannah is a bestselling craft and baking author, a hugely creative stylist and presenter. She runs the beautiful creative blog CoutureCraft.co.uk and is an obsessive instagrammer – come and say hi @CoutureCraft and don't forget to share your *Flowerbomb!* projects using the hashtag #FlowerBombStyle

Her books so far, *Everything Alice*, *Everything Oz* and *Girls' Night In*, have all become global successes. She is passionate about craft and baking, working with brands on developing creative ideas, designing and often presenting them online. She currently holds the coveted title of QVC Craft Ambassador in the UK.

Hannah is from South-East London where she now lives with her beautiful son and handsome husband. She continues to work from her kitchen table creating ideas for her clients – in fact, she's probably there right now!